MONEY, POWER, GREED:
Has the Church Been Sold Out?

JOHN M. MONTGOMERY

Regal Books
A Division of GL Publications
Ventura, California, U.S.A.

Published by Regal Books
A Division of GL Publications
Ventura, California 93006
Printed in U.S.A.

1 2 3 4 5 6 7 8 9 10 / 91 90 89 88 87

Library of Congress Cataloging-in-Publication Data applied for.

Rights for publishing this book in other languages are contracted by Gospel
Literature International (GLINT) foundation. GLINT also provides technical
help for the adaptation, translation, and publishing of Bible study resources
and books in scores of languages worldwide. For further information, contact
GLINT, Post Office Box 488, Rosemead, California, 91770, U.S.A., or the
publisher.

Dedication

Over the last six years many people have helped to bring this book to its final stage. I couldn't begin to name all who have contributed. I am sure that many fine authors will see some of their own words in this book. If I have failed to give credit where credit is due, forgive me, it has not been by intent.

I want to give thanks to my wife who keeps me humble yet lifts me up; to Lowell Jones, my good friend and anchor; to Pastor Bill Johnson and the flock of Calvary Chapel, Weaverville, California, who make Christ truly the Head of the Body.

Contents

Preface
The "Glitter Gospel" in Peril

In writing this book I had been clinically careful to avoid using names of ministers or ministries in a negative way. I felt that the sickness itself should be addressed, not those who were afflicted. It was my belief that a minister's personal life was between himself and his God, and his morals and personality were not something I should expose in diagnosing the ailment that afflicted the Church. I believe my decision was right; however, after this book was in the hands of the publisher, I watched the media contribute to the fall of one Glitter Gospel star and tarnish the names of several other TV ministers and ministries.

Newspapers, magazines, and TV delved into every sordid aspect of the fallen preacher. Television newscasters devoted more time to the battle of the evangelists than they did to the nation's budget deficit or international disarmament. They reported how the attorney for the accused evangelist complained that another TV evangelist was attempting to "take over," the very successful TV

The world . . . looks upon Christians as either the biggest suckers or the worst crooks."

ministry. They quoted the attorney as saying: "If he says any more, we are going to be compelled to show that there is smelly laundry in his hamper."[1]

The media devoted full pages to a sexual affair the superstar had had several years earlier—this man who was the head of a ministry that was valued at close to $200 million. Not only was his sexual affair discussed in detail, his wife's prescription drug addiction, which in other celebrities would normally be presented with a sense of sympathy, was described in a way that made readers even more suspicious of televangelists. In most of the articles the lifestyles of all TV evangelists—their homes, cars, and opulence—were cast in the Elmer-Gantry syndrome in order to humiliate and destroy them.

The Bakker scandal hit the media shortly after Oral Roberts told his television viewers that God was going to call him home by April 1 unless they donated eight million dollars to his ministry. The media had a witch hunt. The *U.S. News and World Report* told of another star of the Glitter Gospel who was offering a paper prayer rug for a donation of $10 or more. The prayer rug article was headlined "Holy Hoaxers" and told of the evangelist sending more than 122,000 letters to his "flock," telling them how they will have health, prosperity, and miracles by using these rugs, all for a seed faith gift of $10.[2]

Another TV evangelist would send a small cloth—which he had prayed over—that recipients could place on their bodies and receive healing and prosperity—but only if they sent a faith pledge to his ministry.

Is it any wonder the media jump on this sort of thing? Can we blame them for our peccadillos?

The world, upon reading these revelations, looks upon Christians as either the biggest suckers or the worst crooks. As an example of how the world views religious fund raising, we need only look at a recent Gallup poll revealing that 40 percent of Americans think religious fundraising tactics are unethical. A national survey, reported in the March 31, 1987, edition of the *Los Angeles Times*, stated that, according to the new survey, preachers in the nation's $2 billion a year television ministries are considered to be more greedy than other clergy, more hypocritical, and less religious.[3]

How can the public hold such a view? Read on. Within the pages of this little book you may find some things that will bother you concerning how the Body of Christ goes about raising money for "God's ministry." However, I believe we can turn the situation around. One author has said that "God is shaking His Church." Then he asks, "How will we respond?"[4] I believe, along with this author, that we can learn from the mistakes the Church has made recently as well as from those which God's people made during Old Testament times.

The Church must learn that when we conform to the methods and hype of Madison Avenue we conform to the ways of the world. These methods are not of God, and He will not honor them in the end. How important is a giant mailing list to a God who is so personal He knows the number of hairs on our heads? How does He feel about our using these mailing lists to peddle paper prayer rugs or healing and prospering cloths to raise money to build bigger and fancier buildings? All this must be an abomination to our Lord who knows when even a sparrow falls.

The publicizing of recent events has shown us that when God's people resort to the methods of the world to raise funds we are but a step away from conforming to the world in our moral standards. The purpose of this book is to present some action which the Church can take to get us back to where we can say, with the psalmist:

I know that you are pleased with me, for my
enemy does not triumph over me. In my integrity you uphold me and set me in your presence
forever (Ps. 41:11-12, *NIV*).

1

Don't Muddy the Water. Things are Good!

W hat does he want with more? At last count the king already has 40,000 horses, with 12,000 horsemen to ride them." Ben-Deker of Makaz, one of Solomon's 12 deputies, was talking to his friend Ben-Heser of the land of Hepher. They had just left a meeting of the deputies during which Solomon had told them he was going to increase taxation on the people so that he could raise more money. Yet Solomon was already wealthier than anyone on earth had ever been before.

Solomon inherited the great kingdom from David, his father. Since becoming Israel's monarch, Solomon had increased the boundaries of the country so that now it extended from the Euphrates River to the land of the Philistines and south to Egypt's border.

He was not yet 30 years old when he became king. With sincere humility he had asked God for wisdom and knowledge to rule the mighty kingdom. These God had given him; and because Solomon had not asked for them,

God had also granted him great wealth. Surrounding nations, concerned for their safety, had welcomed the new king with gifts—and idol-worshiping brides. It was not long before the world was singing of Solomon's greatness, wisdom, and wealth.

Solomon soon became accustomed to the riches God had given him. He began to spend it—first on himself, then later on God. In Solomon's palace, which took 13 years to build, there was a huge ivory throne, overlaid in pure gold. All of his dining service was made of solid gold. Silver was as common as stones in Jerusalem. One room in the palace measured 150 feet long, 75 feet wide and 45 feet high. He built palaces for his wives that were similarly elegant. And to finance it all he taxed his people more and more.

These were some of the things that came to mind the day Ben-Deker and Ben-Heser stood in Jerusalem discussing Solomon's latest decision concerning taxation.

"I'm not sure the people will stand much more. It's not only high taxation. The people can even appreciate the king's lavish expenditures and the fact that he has great stores of gold and silver in the treasury. What is causing much discontent among our people," Ben-Heser added, "is how he uses their money in his personal life." Ben-Heser read from a note he held in his hand. "His 700 wives, 300 concubines, soldiers and servants require 300 bushels of flour, 600 bushels of meal, 10 fat oxen, 20 pasture-fed oxen, 100 sheep and many, many deer, elk and fowls *every single day!* The people resent supporting wives and concubines the king has collected from countries that should be our enemies. Did you know that he not only has built temples for their gods but he even allows the worship of their idols right there in the palace?"

Ben-Deker replied, "He certainly is a far cry from the

spiritual giant his father was. King David never submitted to idol worship nor permitted our people to do so."

Deja Vu

The scene changes. The year is 1987, the country is not Israel, but America. The news media has just released details of the most recent extravagances of a world-renown spiritual leader. The headlines read: "Park That PTL Built Rides Roller-Coaster of Success, Scandal":

> Billboards with the smiling faces of Jim and Tammy Faye Bakker guide visitors along the 15 miles from Charlotte, N.C., to a woodsy, inspirational park here created by the scandal-blemished evangelist. [1]

We are all by now aware of the disgrace the Christian community suffered when the media first revealed that a leading television evangelist had purchased a $440,000 condominium for his and his wife's personal use. As time went on we discovered from the media that this was only the tip of the iceberg.

Among the unrestrained excesses was a remodeled dressing room for guests on his TV broadcast that included a "habitat." What's a habitat? you ask. Well, a habitat is an enclosed area that simulates various environments. The area can be used as a sauna, a sun room, or a rain forest at the push of a button. This particular habitat had such features as a warm breeze, variable temperature shower massage, cypress deck heat lamps to warm the towels, and an AM/FM stereo cassette player. The whirlpool had gold-plated legs; the two basins, gold-plated fixtures; the antique bathtub, polished gold legs; the pull-chain toilet sported gold-plated hardware.

Just a short time prior to this exposure, this evangelist had alerted his "partners" by mail and on TV that the ministry was facing an impending "financial crisis," and the people needed to send more funds. However, during the "financial crisis" the leaders of the ministry took a personal tour to Europe; 10 of them traveled first-class jet—Concord, no less—from New York to Paris at a cost of $1,906 per person. When the media latched onto the story they made public many extravagances that would have fit right in with Solomon's life-style.

Meanwhile, the little people, who most likely worked very hard for their money, continued to send in their tithes and offerings to a ministry they believed was using God's money in a wise and prudent way.

When does the ministry God gives us become ours rather than God's? What causes "things" to become so important that we put them ahead of God? It is true that Solomon built a magnificent Temple for the Lord God—along with the temples he built for his wives' gods. And the TV evangelist also can show many things he did that gave glory and honor to God. But in the lives of both men, "things" began to overshadow God and His message. Both men "taxed" their people so that they could live the life-style they believed befitted their positions.

"Keep the Charge of the Lord"

The mighty King Solomon was the son of King David. God had described David as "a man after my own heart" because David's primary concern during his life was what God wanted. When David lay dying he blessed Solomon with these words:

To us, integrity should certainly mean that we are to be ethical in our personal and professional affairs."

> I am going the way of all the earth. Be strong, therefore, and show yourself a man. And keep the charge of the Lord your God, to walk in His ways, to keep His statutes, His commandments, His ordinances, and His testimonies, according to what is written in the law of Moses, that you may succeed in all that you do and wherever you turn (1 Kings 2:2-3).

Solomon loved God and walked in the statutes of his father (see 1 Kings 3:3). However, as King Solomon grew older and more powerful and more affluent, he seemed to have difficulty living up to his father's charge and conforming to David's sense of personal integrity. David always worked at being honorable. In one of his psalms he cried out to God:

> Vindicate me, O LORD, for I have walked in my integrity; and I have trusted in the LORD without wavering. Examine me, O LORD, and try me; test my mind and my heart. For Thy lovingkindness is before my eyes, and I have walked in Thy truth. I do not sit with deceitful men, nor will I go with pretenders. I hate the assembly of evildoers, and will not sit with the wicked (Ps. 26:1-5).

Integrity, in David's eyes, meant being true to God and true to himself as God made him.

To us, integrity should certainly mean that we are to be ethical in our personal and professional affairs. The sad part is that even though we have the lessons of history to guide us, it appears we have not learned. Solomon, despite his failures, was a powerful monarch, and as long as he kept his eyes on God he prospered in every way. In one of his proverbs he said: "He who walks in integrity walks securely, but he who perverts his ways will be found out" (Prov. 10:9). And, as we read a little farther into the life of Solomon, we discover that he *did* pervert his ways and he *was* found out. History—and Scripture—should have taught us a lesson.

What Difference Does It Make?

Solomon took what his father had accomplished and multiplied it many times. For the first time in their history, the people of Israel had peace, they were living well, they had abundance. They reasoned, "Since things are so good, God must approve of the king and his ways. Don't muddy the water. Leave things the way they are."

That day in Israel, Ben-Deker and Ben-Heser came to the same conclusion: "What does it matter if the king bends a few of God's laws and allows a little false worship because of his many wives? After all, is it so important to be so rigid in all the things God has asked? What could be wrong with bending the law a little here and a little there? If it pleases one of the king's wives, is it wrong to give recognition to Ashtoreth, the fertility goddess of the Phoenicians? All of Solomon's deputies know there is only one God. Solomon knows there is only one God. Recognizing Molech, the god of the Ammonites, and Chemosh, the god of the Moabites is only a political expediency. No one of any importance in the kingdom believes in them. These little inconsistencies are necessary to keep the peace throughout the world." It was just a little thing that had crept into the king's life. What difference did it make? He was still a good king. He was still good for the people. And God was still blessing them with prosperity.

So, the people did not rebel against Solomon's lavish expenditures because they had also begun to worship the good life. They too had sold themselves to other gods— the gods of materialism and abundance. The trappings of materialism and social acceptability, and the fact that they now had peace instead of continual war, had allowed them to overlook Solomon's failure to hear and obey God's voice. They tolerated the high taxation and Solomon's huge expenditures on things that honored the king and dishonored God. After all, God had given Solomon all his wealth, along with his great wisdom. "What difference does it make?"

In 1 Kings 11:6 and 11, however, we find that it made a lot of difference. God said:

> And Solomon did what was evil in the sight of the LORD, and did not follow the Lord fully, as David his father had done . . . . The LORD said to Solomon, "Because you have done this, and you have not kept My covenant and My statutes, which I have commanded you, I will surely tear the kingdom from you, and will give it to your servant."

Was it because of Solomon's great wealth that God was angry? No, God has no problem with His people being rich. He gave Solomon great riches, and He had also given many of His servants wealth in earlier years—Abraham for example; and He does not withhold wealth from His people today.

Wealth and the "good life" do not separate man from God; rather, it is the distraction wealth often causes. God expects to be put first. First before what? Surely, peace, contentment and material things must be important to

God! These good things the people of Israel were enjoying must have been from him, so He must have approved of what Solomon was doing, we rationalize.

The problem was, Solomon became distracted by his wealth and power. Even though he had great wisdom and, like us, the lessons of history and the Word of God to guide him, the Bible tells us that he did not learn from his wisdom, history, or God's Word. He still allowed his 700 wives and 300 concubines to turn "his heart away" from the Lord, especially in his old age (1 Kings 11:3-4).

Yes, God had blessed Solomon with wealth and power. But there was a condition to these gifts: Solomon had to use his blessings for God's glory, not for his own. The gold and silver belonged to God, and they still do, nothing has changed. We may hold onto our wealth for a while, but it does not belong to us. It was Solomon's responsibility, and it is the responsibility of every one of us, to manage what God gives us and not get so attached to things that we forget they do not belong to us.

Jesus said, in His Sermon on the Mount, "You cannot serve both God and Money" (Matt. 6:24, *NIV*). God loves us, but the Scriptures tell us that He is a jealous God. When we serve money we become guilty of idolatry; when we put things ahead of God, He becomes jealous.

It seems paradoxical for us to talk of heaven but strive for things. Jesus was not guilty of this dual system of values. He did not put materialism ahead of the kingdom.

A Watchman for God

The prophet Ezekiel, whom God called "a watchman for the house of Israel," was sent to tell the religious leaders of his day that God was not happy with how they were behaving. Ezekiel obeyed the Lord and sounded the alarm. "God is ready to judge you," he said over and over. The leaders paid no attention to these serious words from the prophet because "their hearts [were] greedy for unjust gain." So God told Ezekiel to tell his countrymen:

> Woe, shepherds of Israel who have been feeding themselves! Should not the shepherds feed the flock? You eat the fat and clothe yourselves with the wool, you slaughter the fat sheep without feeding the flock. Those who are sickly you have not strengthened, the diseased you have not healed, the broken you have not bound up, the scattered you have not brought back, nor have you sought for the lost; but with force and with severity you have dominated them. And they scattered for lack of a shepherd, and they became food for every beast of the field and . . . there was no one to seek for them (Ezek. 34:2-6).

The shepherds did not listen to the prophet. God had already explained that, to these religious leaders, Ezekiel was "nothing more than one who sings love songs with a beautiful voice and plays an instrument well, for they hear your words but do not put them into practice" (Ezek. 33:32, NIV).

It is never easy to reveal the wrongdoings of a fellow pastor, evangelist, teacher, or other leader. Sometimes we hesitate to denounce sin in a fellow Christian because we reason that, after all, none of us is perfect. Besides, we don't want to be guilty of compromising someone else's testimony. Anyhow, God seems to be blessing our brother; just look how the money is rolling in and the ministry is growing. Who am I to question or criticize one of

_____

God wants to bless us . . . but He has
one requirement: He wants to be in charge."

_____

God's servants? People might think I'm just jealous.

It is true that it is good for us to be discreet; discretion prevents us from accusing or gossiping. However, the world and the Prince of this world are not discreet. The truth will eventually come out, then the media will make the most of the "scandal." The world is always alert to our shortcomings and Satan is always ready to accuse us. Those of us who preach the Truth, must live the truth, or be guilty of preaching emptiness. We must be watchmen for God. Peter tells us that false teachers among us will "follow their sensuality, and because of them the way of the truth will be maligned; and in their greed they will exploit you with false words" (2 Pet. 2:2-3).

Concealed and tolerated sin will eventually destroy our witness and our testimony, and when one member of the Body is disgraced, all members suffer. All of us sin and fall short of God's mark; however, God says that we must all confess our sin and deal with our shortcomings openly.

Our God wants to bless us. He does not slight those who put Him first. He wants us to have abundance in our ministries and in our lives. But He has one requirement: He wants to be in charge.

2

Who's in Charge Here?

Over the past few years the media has delighted in the battle that is taking place in many denominations regarding who owns the church real estate. Does the local congregation own the property or does the denomination? The *Presbyterian Layman* of May 1980, said:

> The Supreme Court of the United States in a decision given July 2, 1979, concerning who owns church property has created a difficult problem for the United Presbyterian Church. For years the Presbyterian family of churches has operated under the implied trustee principle in regard to local church property. This policy served the church well and gave it unity, vitality, and influence beyond its members and contributed to its strength. The Supreme Court since the July, 1979, decision holds that the denomination cannot hold claim to local church prop-

erty unless it is stated in the constitution that
the local church property belongs to the parent
church. This puts the church at large in a difficult dilemma. For if it owns local church property then it is also responsible and can be held
liable for what the local church does.[1]

Can you see that the problem as outlined by the article
is not the real problem at all? Should not the parent church
feel responsible for the local church regardless of the legal
ramifications? Are we so fractured that each part of the
Body feels no responsibility for the other part?

The Head Bone Connected to the Neck Bone . . .

Notice that the article states that the parent church and
local church had unity before. It appears that they were
united only as long as neither felt responsibility for the
other.
  The article continues:

We should ask ourselves whether legal title to
local church property is too great a risk for the
denomination to take. It could bring troubles
that it does not want, and should not be called
to bear. It might make the church at large liable
in case of financial failure on the part of a local
church, or perhaps in case of negligence where
injury or death occurred. Related church properties should enter into our decision also.
Retirement church homes are a case in point.
We are aware of the plight of the Methodist
homes in California. They have been sued for
breach of contract. It is possible that the United

Methodist Church will have to pay the damages.[2]

Certainly we can all see the potential problems this article outlines. But can we as a whole Body accept the attitude: "OK, local church. You have a problem. But don't expect help from us. We are too big and important to risk helping you"? When we start to protect ourselves to the detriment of our brothers and sisters in the Lord our priorities are very confused.

The article made reference to Methodist retirement homes in California, that the United Methodist Church would have to step to the line and pay the bills. Why shouldn't the church feel a responsibility to pay the bills, whether or not the courts demand it? Debts were incurred, craftsmen and laborers did their work, supply houses furnished products, contractors expended money so that the retirement homes could be built. All the work was done in the belief that the church would pay its bills.

What is the alternative? Bankruptcy? Although most churches balk at the idea of declaring bankruptcy, some still take this method of avoiding paying their bills.

What do the Scriptures say about this practice? Psalm 37:21 says, "The wicked borrows and does not pay back, but the righteous is gracious and gives." What kind of a witness does a church present to the world if it neglects to pay its just debts?

While the battle goes on, the media exposes and magnifies it.

In the Bank We Trust

How do we get into situations such as these? When Jesus warned His followers about the cost of discipleship He prefaced His warning with these words:

> Which one of you, when he wants to build a
> tower, does not first sit down and calculate the
> cost, to see if he has enough to complete it?
> Otherwise, when he has laid a foundation, and
> is not able to finish, all who observe it begin to
> ridicule him, saying, "This man began to build
> and was not able to finish" (Luke 14:28-30).

Yet, churches are guilty of doing just that. They use
the devil's tool of rationalization: "We need a bigger facility
right now. After all, it will only cost more later on. And
God will provide if we only step out in faith." How does
this fit in with what Jesus said about counting the cost
before we take on a project?

"Five acres may be big enough now, but what about
five years from now. Shouldn't we look to the future and
buy ten acres? Of course we can't afford it, but God will
provide. We just need to step out in faith."

The problem is, these churches seldom step out in
faith in God; rather they use the world's means of provid-
ing. It has always seemed strange to me that when we
have a major project we go to the Lord and ask that His
will be done; then before the amens are over we run to the
bank for a loan. It appears that we trust the money lenders
more than we trust the Lord. "Ah, yes," you say, "but
God provides the means to pay the lender." If we believe
that God can provide the money *after* we have borrowed
it, why can we not trust Him to bring it in before we go
into debt? When we pray to God, asking Him to provide,
then borrow our money from the bank, we are taking away
His privilege to answer our prayers.

If my son came to me and asked me for a car he really

We in the Church go to our Father with our needs; then we satisfy our needs through . . . bank loans. We give lip service to God Almighty, but put our trust in the god Mammon."

---

needed, because I love my son I would very seriously consider giving him what he needed. I would begin to plan financially to provide him with a car. But what if he asked me and, before I could get the car for him, he borrowed money from the bank for it because he wanted it "right now"? I think my reaction would be not only disappointment but also anger that he did not trust me to provide for him, and that he could not wait long enough for me to answer yes or no.

All too often we in the Church go to our Father with our needs; then we satisfy our needs through credit cards and bank loans. We give lip service to God Almighty, but put our trust in the god Mammon.

Build a Bigger Barn

Another example where a fine ministry got ahead of God is described in a 1973 article in a leading Christian magazine about "one of America's greatest church success stories." The article told how, in a few short years, this church had built a "worldwide reputation." It discussed the many community awards the church had received and said that much of the church's success had to be attributed to the pastor. God was using the pastor to reach great numbers of unchurched with the Good News of Jesus Christ.

In 1973 this ministry was seeking God and was being obedient to His Word. God was first in the life of both the congregation and the pastor. However, even in 1973 the article hinted at potential problems. The article ended with a question and answer format. One of the questions asked of the pastor was, "What about the budget of your church?" The pastor's answer could have tipped us off to future problems in this growing ministry.

I do not believe in a budget. It's a bad word. I am against budgets because they limit God. When God moves in an area, we have to be ready to move with him. Budgets seldom move with God. At [our church] we have no contest or fund raising programs. I will not have any special banquets to raise money. Yet, this year we will probably hit a million dollars in church contributions. That's pretty great when you realize that in 11 years we have come to this point and have no heavy givers.[3]

Sounds pretty good.

Now let's jump ahead to 1979, six short years from the date the article appeared in the magazine. The *Los Angeles Times* says that public record, along with interviews with people who are acquainted with the church's finances, indicate that the church is "suffering a gigantic hangover from a decade" of binge spending. The positive statements the pastor made in 1973 now sound hollow. Requests for money through mass mailings and TV appeals have become a major part of this ministry along with banquets, insurance schemes, etc.

The pastor felt that budgets limit God and he wanted to "move with" God, and, as the article pointed out, moving with God included several attempts to set up a very costly television ministry, establishing a church in another area that was for a time headed by the pastor's 20-year-old son-in-law, and ownership of two church-owned airplanes and a church-supported pilot.[4]

The article takes several pages listing extravagances and discussing the problems of an insolvent trust fund and the legal ramifications of such a trust fund. The article stated that the "insolvency of the trust fund" was typical of

———————————

The Lord Himself made it very clear that
He put good management in a very
special position."

———————————

other financial problems the church had. There was $450,000 worth of overdue bills with a total indebtedness of $5 million. Some of those within the organization blamed this condition on "years of mismanagement, waste and inefficiency."⁵

Another sad tale of getting ahead of God. The pastor is a man of God who got his priorities mixed up.

Is Anybody in Charge Here?

Paul in his letter to Timothy foresaw the problems caused by poor leadership; so he gave Timothy guidelines for elders and deacons. Paul stated that a leader must be "free from the love of money" and able to manage "his own household well," for "if a man does not know how to manage his own household, how will he take care of the church of God?" (1 Tim. 3:3-5).

The Lord Himself made it very clear that He put good management in a very special position. In Luke 16 Jesus said,

> He who is faithful in a very little thing is faithful also in much; and he who is unrighteous in a very little thing is unrighteous also in much. If therefore you have not been faithful in the use of unrighteous Mammon, who will entrust the true riches to you? And if you have not been faithful in the use of that which is another's, who will give you that which is your own? No servant can serve two masters; for either he will hate the one, and love the other, or else he will hold to one, and despise the other. You cannot serve God and Mammon (vv. 10-13).

The aforementioned ministry seems to have failed to heed the words of Scripture about the wise use of money and about going in debt.

During this ministry's time of rapid growth, the church started a three-story building at an estimated cost in excess of one million dollars. The work was halted in 1979 with the building far from complete. (The building is still not complete at the time of this writing.) Because of inflation it will now cost almost as much to complete the building as it was to have cost to build it in the first place. Perhaps the building was needed at the time it was started (although many felt it was a monument to man). However, with all the other problems in the church—financial and otherwise, the timing was obviously wrong. It was not God's timing. Had the pastor believed in budgets, and had he listened to wise counsel, perhaps his church would not have been an example of folly and mismanagement to the world and the Christian Body.

But, praise God, that is not the end to this story. The August 1987, edition of *Charisma* Magazine reports that "after a decade of controversy, the once high-profile church is seeking a fresh start." The pastor of this congregation of fewer than 3,000, down from 15,000 in the early 1970s, says that he has had "a fresh vision from the Lord about where we're headed." The church's problems are not over. They are still involved in legal problems. But they are now looking to God for a way out. [6]

In the next chapter we will discuss another problem about authority which churches today face.

3

I Demand My Rights!

Whenever the subject of separation of church and state comes up, Christian churches are the ones who holler the loudest for freedom of religion. And rightly so. But, how often do we abuse this freedom and the intent of our Constitutional rights?

> Bishop H. Carlisle Estes poured goblets of "sacramental" wine. His partner, Cardinal Vincent J. Morino, took guests' orders—for sirloin tips with mushrooms, roast duckling or scallops sauteed in chablis. In the kitchen, the mother superior prepared the feast. Hailing the "divine service" as a "triumph of good over evil," Estes asked dinner guests to "donate" $15—tax deductible—for the upkeep of his controversial Temple of Bacchus.[1]

The founders of the Temple of Bacchus have lost a

long legal battle with the town of Wells, Maine, over whether their Temple of Bacchus is a church or a restaurant. They had made the premises available to the public through advertisement and provided the public with food, drink and entertainment in exchange for "donations." The judge in the case agreed with the town, noting that the nature of the activities carried on inside the building, rather than the name on the outside, determines whether or not it is a church.[2]

Who Controls the Purse Strings?

In California, the attorney general attempted to take over the assets of a church of around 100,000 members. The church's annual income is in excess of $70 million, tax free money. Its members are required to give their first tithe to the church; they are expected to set aside a second tithe for their own use, that being their personal expenses for spiritual enjoyment in attending church festivals. Of course, the church also receives the money from the annual festivals. Every third year the members are expected to cough up a third tithe for the support of widows, orphans and the poor of the church. Sounds good to me, how about you?

The state, however, took a dim view of how the money from the tithes was actually used, since the church members never received a financial accounting, nor was there ever an audit taken and reported to the members, the state, or to the IRS.

The legal problems of this church boiled down to a simple matter of who controlled the purse strings. The state contended that the church held its assets as a charitable trust; therefore, the state had the right to examine the church finances in the same way they oversaw the conduct of other charities operating within the state. The attorney general counted upon a little used section of the code that allowed the state to put every church in the position of a charitable trust. However, recent legislation changed this right to the extent that the state, before examining the finances of a church or putting the church under their authority, first had to prove there was wrongdoing on the part of the church. They had to prove that the church was in violation of the law.

The state has argued that the first amendment guarantee of freedom of religion does not excuse the perpetration of fraud in the name of religion. Nor does it shield the perpetrators from corrective action in the courts. In the case of the church in question, the state contended that church officials were siphoning off church funds for their personal use, and that the pastor accepted money far too lavishly, and that the pastor's chief advisor, with a salary exceeding $200,000 per year, was unduly benefiting from his position. This advisor also had an unlimited expense account, homes in Beverly Hills and Pasadena, California, and one in Tucson, Arizona. All of these homes were initially financed by the church.

The state has also alleged other extravagances. For example, giant credit card excesses, such as $22,571 at one Paris hotel, purchases of antiques, paintings and extremely lavish gifts. The state claimed that it was attempting to correct alleged fraudulent diversion of assets by the church's leadership. The attorney general charged that, since 1975, church leaders have diverted at least one million dollars annually. Can you see the problem developing?

Let us, for the sake of discussion, assume that the state's allegation is true; that the leadership is in fact diverting these large sums of money for their own gain; that excessive spending by the pastor and his chief advisor is in fact taking place. Attorneys for the church have said,

> It is not the business of the state to regulate the pastor or how he chooses to spread the Gospel. If he wants to speak to world leaders, travel in first-class sections of airlines or travel by private jet and stay in luxury hotels, so be it . . . . The membership of the church has been amply informed of these things, . . . and if they don't like it they can stop tithing and leave the church.[3]

Now, if we agree with the attorneys and decide that the state or federal government must not, under any circumstances, become involved in the affairs of any church, no matter what the church is doing, do we not open the door to every type of crook and charlatan who is out to rip off whoever they can in the name of the church? Yet, if the state is allowed to regulate the activities of the church, any church, could this be the first step toward state control of the church?

The final determination on this case denied the state the freedom to examine the church in question, and in fact made it very difficult for the state or federal government to get involved in the financial affairs or have access to financial records of any church unless they first prove wrongdoing on the part of the church. I leave the right or wrong of this decision to you. I am sure you can see the potential threat either way. The pity is that the problem ever had to rise at all. No matter which way it goes, those of us who are in the Body of Christ are made to look bad.

The United States Constitution, through the First Amendment, gives individuals the freedom to hold any religious belief . . . . But it does not guarantee us unlimited right to act as we wish."

Hiding Under the Amendments

Christians—that is, true believers—have no intention of violating the law, nor do they intend to be poor witnesses. Many of them have, however, been duped into following the tricky ways of the devil because they have not taken the time to know or understand the law. Our laws were originally not intended by God or the government to hurt or hinder churches; rather they were formulated to protect both the state and the church. Paul told the Romans:

> Rulers are not a cause of fear for good behavior, but for evil. Do you want to have no fear of authority? Do what is good, and you will have praise from the same; for it is a minister of God to you for good. But if you do what is evil, be afraid; for it does not bear the sword for nothing; for it is a minister of God, an avenger who brings wrath upon the one who practices evil (13:3-4).

If we, the Church, do not take the time to know and understand the law, we will be guilty of violations and, in time, will bring upon ourselves and our church the scorn of governing authorities.

The United States Constitution, through the First Amendment, gives individuals the freedom to hold any religious belief they wish. But it does not guarantee us unlimited right to act as we wish. The Supreme Court has stated:

> The First Amendment embraces two concepts: the freedom to believe and the freedom to act. The first, the freedom to believe is absolute.

But in the nature of things, the second, the
freedom to act, cannot be. It is the freedom to
act that remains subject to regulations for the
protection of society.[4]

Any violation of the law by the corporate church or by
individuals responsible for the leadership of the church is
an "act." To attempt to hide under the cover of the First
or the Fourteenth Amendment is a violation of the charge
the Apostle Peter gave us:

Submit yourselves for the Lord's sake to every
human institution: whether to a king as the one
in authority; or to governors as sent by him for
the punishment of evildoers and the praise of
those who do right. For such is the will of God
that by doing right you may silence the ignorance of foolish men (1 Pet. 2:13-15).

A Church by Any Other Name . . .

The organized church today faces a crisis because the government is forced to increase its control of "churches"
because of abuse. Much has been written regarding the
separation of church and state; the First Amendment is a
concern of every thinking Christian. Yet, because
"churches" are being formed under the umbrella of religious freedom solely for purposes of tax exemption, it is
necessary for governmental authority to take appropriate
action. In order to better determine the legitimacy of
"churches," all organized churches now need to complete
forms, exemption applications, etc. Because of this action
as well as other perceived threats to our religious freedom

we tend to regard the state as our enemy.

Many warnings have been sounded concerning the government's interest in the organization and operation of churches. One example of such a warning is from the *Fordham Law Review of 1977,* volume 45:

> In the last thirty years congress has introduced a large number of religious distinctions into the Internal Revenue Code. These distinctions do not relate to the content of any religion or church belief. Such distinctions would obviously be unconstitutional. Rather, these distinctions are organizational. They relate to the structures and functions of the various types of religious organizations, especially churches. Many of these distinctions draw lines based upon the degree of churchiness or church relatedness of an organization. Churches, by the very fact that they are churches, are exempt from the Internal Revenue Code Section 501c3. The term *church* is and has been very important to Federal tax laws since 1950. Yet, today there is still no regulation explaining the difference between a religious organization that is a church and one that is not a church.[5]

To the public at large, all church and church organizations fall under the category of "religious" and, therefore, all are suspect. What has caused the public at large to look with such criticism upon religious organizations? Does the corporate Christian church bring this criticism upon itself? Have we fallen into the trap of becoming servants of the institutions of Christendom instead of servants of Christ? Are we guilty of confusing Christendom with Christianity. Do we know the difference?

If we are careful to serve Christ, not the creation of man, then we will have no problem with what the Apostle Paul told us to do: "render to all [governing authorities] what is due them" (Rom. 13:7).

Malcolm Muggeridge, in his little book *The End of Christendom*, explains the difference:

> Christendom, however, is something quite different from Christianity, being the administrative or power structure based on the Christian religion and constructed by men. The founder of Christianity was, of course, Christ. The founder of Christendom I suppose could be named as the Emperor Constantine . . . It is not Christ's Christianity that is now floundering. You might even say that Christ abolished Christendom before it began by stating thatHis kingdom was not of this world. [6]

If we are careful to serve Christ, not the creation of man, then we will have no problem with what the Apostle Paul told us to do, which is to "render to all [governing authorities] what is due them" (Rom. 13:7).

There are a great many churches in the United States that could be referred to as "gimmick" churches, those organized for the sole purpose of allowing their members to avoid paying taxes. Let's assume that it is the other guy who is causing most of the problems between church and state, the "other guy" being the gimmick churches.

How does the Internal Revenue Service view these organized "churches"? This is subject for discussion in the next chapter.

4

"Beauty" in the Eyes of the IRS

Kirby J. Hensley, self-proclaimed reverend and leader of the World Wide Universal Life Church, maintains that the only tenet of the church he heads is:

> . . . doing what is right and that all the people have the right to determine what beliefs are right for them as long as they do not interfere with the rights of others.[1]

The Universal Life Church, according to Hensley, now has a membership of over seven million, all ordained! Now, why would seven million people become ordained ministers in an organization that has no real belief? The answers can be found in headlines of a tabloid sold in supermarket checkout stands throughout the country: "Millions Can Avoid Tax Through Legal Loophole." The subtitle states, "Anyone earning $20,000 per year can do it." The article spells out in detail how not to pay taxes, and it tells the readers how to get ordained, then how to turn their houses into churches.

> There is nothing to stop every one of the 7 million members from taking out one of our church charters and turning his house into a church and being tax exempt.[2]

The attorney for the Universal Life Church, in the same article, comments:

> It's a definite possibility that all the homes in the U.S. could be turned into churches. But I see nothing wrong with this suggestion. Nor do I see anything to stop it.[3]

I am happy to say that it has been stopped to a great extent. The IRS is cracking down on how the members of the church form their own churches, and they are doing so with the blessings of the court.

A recent court ruling (Tax Court Memo 1978-149) states:

> Mr. Pat Heller was ordained by a mail order church, the Church of the Tolerance. Mr. Heller then formed the Church of External Life and Liberty. The church had six members. [By the way, the six members were members of his own family.] Heller's donations, which he deducted from his income tax return, constituted the church's only income. The church paid the rent and the utilities on his apartment. The IRS disallowed the charitable deduction. The

tax court determined that what emerges from
the facts before us is an organization controlled
by the petitioner and functioned to serve his
personal living needs. Insofar as we can determine and discern, the principle purpose of the
church is to provide the petitioner with the
means for his claiming deductions for his own
personal living expenses. This private inure-
ment prescribed by section 170(c2c) disqualifies
his gifts to the church from being charitable contributions. Deductions for such contributions
therefore must be denied.[4]

Kirby and his gimmick church has sold a bill of goods to
thousands of people who believe that by doing what Kirby
recommends they will avoid taxes. The courts have said it
will not work, but the hype goes on and the people continue to try, and they continue to send in their dollars to
Kirby.

Will the Real Church Please Stand Up?

You might ask, "Why don't *they* stop the crooks?" Part of
the reason the crooks have not been stopped is because
the crooks know the law as it pertains to IRS Section
501c3 far better than the leadership of the Body of Christ
knows it. Thus they are able to bend the rules, and if the
law cracks down on the crooks, it will also have to crack
down on legitimate churches.

Another reason the crooks have been able to operate
so effectively is that the term *church* has never been
defined by either the state or the IRS. The Internal Revenue News Release IR1930 states:

Since beliefs and practices are so varied, the
IRS cannot define a church, and must resort to
a case by case approach to determine whether
any organization is a church.[5]

The IRS looks at 14 elements to determine if in fact an
organization is a church. Every church leader needs to be
aware of these elements; the gimmick church leaders are.
The church is required to have:
1. A distinct legal existence
2. A recognized creed and form of worship
3. A definite and distinct ecclesiastical government
4. A formal code of doctrine and disciplines
5. A distinct religious history
6. A membership not associated with any other
   church or denomination
7. A complete organization of ordained ministers
   ministering to that congregation
8. Ordained ministers selected after completing prescribed courses of study
9. A literature of its own
10. Established places of worship
11. Regular congregations
12. Regular religious services
13. Sunday School for the religious instruction of the
    young
14. Schools for the preparation of its ministers.[6]

The IRS expects an organization which calls itself a
church to meet most of these 14 requirements. The guidelines emphasize that structure, not religious content, is
the most important aspect in the eyes of the IRS.

It is apparent that the above criteria favors the frame-
work of the denominational church or large organizational
church, and eliminates smaller, independent churches.

This problem is discussed in a publication called "What Is a Church—The Dilemma of the Para-Church," put out by The Center for Law and Religious Freedom in Oak Park, Illinois.

> The simplistic solution to the problem would be to call a moratorium on the granting of tax exemptions unless the organization has already been established a set number of years, say fifty.[7]

Such a solution is not compatible with the fundamental Christian value of regeneration. The forming of new local bodies of believers would stop, and we would end up with a church very much like a state church. The writer of this "solution" knows that this approach will not work but is pointing out just how far the state might go in order to stop the crooks and charlatans from using the umbrella of the church for their own profit.

"Greet the Church That Is in Their House"

How would the church at Colossae or Philippi stack up against the 14 requirements? Not very well. The elders had no formal courses of study; no literature—other than the Old Testament; no schools for preparing their ministers; and the members met in homes.

Churches seeking IRS exemption today would not only have to meet most of the 14 IRS guidelines, they would also, in all probability, need to answer a series of questions aimed, it appears, at discouraging their continued request for exemption. When a church files an Exemption Form 1023 requesting federal exemption, it now gets a letter from the IRS requesting more information. This letter says, in part:

> Before we can recognize an organization as being exempt from federal income tax we must have enough information to show that all legal requirements have been met. Please send us the requested information within 15 days so we can complete the application on your case. If we do not hear from you within that time [15 days], we will assume that you do not want us to consider the matter further and will close your case. In the event that we do that, we will notify the appropriate state officials as required by section 6104C of the code, that based upon the information we have, we are unable to recognize you as an organization of the type described in section 501c3. If you do not provide the requested information it will be considered by the Internal Revenue Service that you have not taken all reasonable steps to secure the determination under section 7428(b2) of the code. Not taking all reasonable steps in a timely manner to secure the determination may be considered as a failure to exhaust administrative remedies available to you in the service and may preclude the issuance of a declaratory judgment in the matter under judicial proceedings.[8]

Now, let us assume that your fellowship has grown to a size which you feel is sufficient to be called a church. Upon the advice of council you decide that you should seek nonprofit and tax-exempt status. You make application on

Form 1023. In a few weeks you receive a letter including the above considerations. You begin to wonder what the IRS is really seeking and if you will be able to comply within the required 15-day deadline. To many groups, even the language of the letter would be enough to scare them off.

The Ultimate Test

After making their application on Form 1023, a church in Southern California received a letter from the IRS including these questions and instructions:

1. Do you maintain ecclesiastical control over your members?
2. Does the congregation have any control over the pastor, or any say in who he will be?
3. How frequently do you hold services? What are the necessary qualifications to be eligible to conduct the services?
4. Submit a copy of sample sermon, or service.
5. What are the specific beliefs of your organization? Please submit a copy of your tenets or creed.
6. Has your organization established any permanent place of worship? Please submit a description of the facility.
7. Will anyone use your facility other than for a purpose directly carrying out your work? Will any of your directors or employees reside at your facility? If so, explain fully. Is the owner of the facility related to you in any way, other than as a landlord?
8. Does your organization carry out the administration of sacerdotal functions?
9. Does your organization plan to ordain ministers? If so, what are the necessary requirements for a person to become a minister?

10. Is the general public made aware of your religious services? If so, by what means?
11. Will anyone connected with your organization receive a salary or expense money from you? If so, explain fully their names and duties, the number of hours each week that they will work, state the amount of compensation each will receive and the basis for arriving at the amounts of such payments.
12. Does the organization have ordained ministers? What formal training do they have? Please submit copies of your certificates of ordination.
13. What is the present size of your congregation?[9]

Can you imagine Philemon, the pastor of "the church at your house," receiving such a letter? Can you further imagine him responding to such a letter with 15 days?

It should be noted that the bulk of the questions asked of this church were answered within its Articles of Incorporation and By-Laws that were submitted with the application for exemption.

Many of these questions are attempts to weed out those so-called churches that are seeking to avoid taxes by using the church as a tax shelter device (Kirby Hensley and the Universal Life Church, for example).

A Can of Worms?

What are some of the problems the IRS, the states, and local governments must contend with in the Universal Life Church, not to mention the domino effect on the Body of Christ and private citizens in general?

George McClain is a "cardinal" of the Universal Life Church in New York state. McClain had answered a maga-

The Church of the Lord Jesus Christ is to be a 'church in all her glory, having no spot or wrinkle or any such thing; but . . . be holy and blameless" (Eph. 5:27).

zine ad and soon received his ordination from Kirby Hensley. Since his ordination, McClain himself has been involved with the ordination of more than 175,000 "ministers." For several years his church has been entangled in a tax battle with the IRS and New York state. The state has taken the position that his church and those like it are nothing more than an umbrella for tax revolt. This is well described in an article from *Money* Magazine:

Taxpayers are a vanishing breed in some parts of New York state. For example, in Catskill communities like Liberty, tax collectors were once buoyed up by opulent private mansions and resorts. After the Catskills started to fall from tourists' grace, abandoned hotels and other properties were snapped up for tax exempt use by religious or charitable groups .... As the roles of taxpayers shrank, payment for municipal services came from fewer and fewer pockets. Taxes became especially crippling in Hardenborough Township. A virginal region without so much as a village. Many of its 54,000 acres were already in the state's Catskill Forest preserve. Pretty soon, tax exemptions drained 4.8 million dollars of assessed evaluation from what was left of their area. A farmer with an income of $10,000 found himself with an $8,000 property tax bill. In desperation the people of Hardenborough turned to the Universal Life Church. In one day McClain ordained 213 of the town's 236 taxpayers. Church charters followed and a sympathetic tax assessor granted them exemptions.[10]

It is not hard to feel empathy, in fact to sympathize, with the citizens of Hardenborough and other communities that have many exempt property owners within their tax district. Imagine yourself as one of those 236 taxpayers in Hardenborough Township who had to carry the tax burden for the residents of all 54,000 acres. Your taxes have to help pay for fire and police protection, as well as other community services, to hotels, resorts, campgrounds, etc., that are tax exempt. Would you consider looking for ways to reduce your taxes?

Christians and their churches should help find equitable arrangements to help situations such as these, even if it means we have to pay our share of taxes on property that is legally exempt. Christians should be good witnesses and not antagonize those in authority or take advantage of tax breaks at the expense of others. We have within the Body some of the most competent legal advisors which law schools can produce. We need to seek their wise counsel, understand the problems which tax exemptions create for others, and begin to clean up our own house. Not only will this help our witness, it will eliminate having the state or the IRS clean up for us.

Of course, before we can do any of these things we need to realize that the Church of the Lord Jesus Christ is to be a "church in all her glory, having no spot or wrinkle or any such thing; but . . . be holy and blameless" (Eph. 5:27).

I challenge every ministry to begin to strive for the high quality Paul spoke of in Ephesians. Next, every ministry that has major facilities—and there are many—should evaluate the ramifications of their exemption and see if their tax exempt status puts undue strain on the community they serve and to which they witness. If your position causes your community and other taxpayers to bear a greater burden than they should, then sit down with leaders of your community and see how the church can pay its fair share. Such a witness will help to offset the damage the Christian church has suffered as a result of recent bad publicity. Also, we should be careful not to make enemies of those who are responsible for making laws that protect our right to worship freely.

5

We Have Met the Enemy and They Are Us

Does your church have banquets where you ask for a donation? Or musicals or plays where entry is by a ticket designated "donation"? These are just a couple of church fund-raising activities the IRS carefully scrutinizes. How valid are these tactics for a nonprofit organization? What does the law have to say about them?

To keep peace with governing authorities we need to know what is expected of us.

An IRS publication explains it this way:

> If you contributed to a charitable organization and also received a benefit from it, you may deduct only the amount that is more than the value of the benefit you received. If you pay more than fair market value to a qualified organization for merchandise, goods, or services, the amount you pay that is more than the value of the item may be a charitable contribution.

We Christians are the first one to raise a fuss when 'false' churches are organized just to avoid paying taxes . . . . Yet, many Christian organizations use some of the same tactics for some of the same reasons."

Example 1. You pay $20 for a box lunch at a church picnic. If the lunch, plus any entertainment or other services provided, has a fair market value of $6, the excess paid, $14, is a contribution to the church if all the proceeds of the picnic go to the church.[1]

Gospel Peddlers?

We Christians are the first ones to raise a fuss when "false" churches are organized just to avoid paying taxes. These churches give the "true" church a bad name in the way they raise funds and evade taxes. And we wonder why governing authorities let them get away with deceiving the people. Yet, many Christian religious organizations use some of the same tactics for some of the same reasons.

What about the radio and television church that offers a "love gift in return for your support"? Did you also get a letter from a well-known ministry saying: "For your gift of $50.00 or more we'll send you the Bible on tape" or, "For your gift of $25.00 or more we'll send you a King James Red Letter Edition worth $29.95"?

Christianity Today told of an experience Professor Quentin Schultze of Calvin College had. Professor Schultze sent letters to a hundred radio and television ministries in North America, asking for their financial and doctrinal statements. Of course, his name was placed on their mailing lists. Schultze said he received "a foam-rubber hospital slipper, numerous pennies, facial soap, and twigs from the Holy Land," to name a few of the items. However, he received only nine financial statements and fewer statements of doctrine from the ministries.[2]

I once received a newsletter that carried this love-gift concept to its ultimate. The last page of the letter said that for my "donation" of $5.00 they would send me my choice of a number of items. It then went on to say that the larger the "donation," the better the return gift would be. The final offer was that if I would send $500 or more I would receive a video tape deck worth $495. Donation? Who is kidding whom?

How does the IRS determine that these ministries are legitimate but the Temple of Bacchus is not? Is the offer of the Bible on tape or the leather bound red letter edition of the Bible any different in the eyes of the IRS from scallops sauteed in chablis?

If the state does make that determination, what is to prevent it from deciding that the Christian church is in error and the Temple of Bacchus is truly a church? The thing that prevents this discrimination, of course, is the First Amendment. What then can we do to keep the IRS or the state from getting in a position where they must make that kind of judgment? The place to start is to do what the Scripture passage we have already quoted says to do:

> Let every person be in subjection to the governing authorities. For there is no authority except from God, and those which exist are established by God. Therefore he who resists authority has opposed the ordinance of God; and they who have opposed will receive condemnation upon themselves. For rulers are not a cause of fear for good behavior, but for evil. Do you want to have no fear of authority? Do what is good, and you will have praise from the same (Rom. 13:1-3).

Do you want to have no fear of authority? Do what is good, and you will have praise from the same" (Romans 13:3).

Raising funds for God's work in such a manner that we conflict with the laws of the land or that puts our church in a position where our witness is damaged cannot possibly come under the command of God. If Christian ministries make every effort to adhere to the laws governing fundraising for nonprofit organizations, without trying to get around them, we will make a good start at helping the IRS formulate guidelines that will benefit honest churches.

In an article entitled "Financing the Great Commission," David L. McKenna presents an antidote to fundraising abuses. He says that Jesus, in the Parable of the Talents (Matt. 25:14-25), gives us fundamentals for stewardship. (1) We are owners of nothing; all belongs to the Master. (2) We are entrusted with everything; God has entrusted to us His creation. (3) We owe all; the goal and motive of Christian stewardship is giving out of gratitude for God's grace and trust. (4) We invest all; we are expected not only to guard the resources God has given us, we are also to multiply them. (5) We serve all; we are responsible to share our resources. (6) We are accountable to God, as the servants were accountable to the absentee landlord. (7) We are rewarded by God; joy is the personal reward for good, faithful and effective stewardship.[3]

In the same issue of this magazine, the financing methods of George Müeller, a nineteenth-century British evangelist who founded four orphanages, are described. Of course, by today's standards these guidelines would be almost impossible to follow. They are:

1. No funds should ever be solicited. No facts or figures concerning needs are to be revealed by the workers in the orphanage to anyone, except to God in prayer.

2. No debts should ever be incurred.

3. Money contributed for a specific purpose should

never be used for any other purpose.

4. All accounts should be audited annually by professional auditor.

5. No ego-pandering by publications of donors' names with the amount of their gifts; each donor should be thanked privately.

6. No "names" of prominent or titled persons should be sought for the board or to advertise the institution.

7. The success of the institution should be measured not by the numbers served or by the amounts of money taken in, but by God's blessing on the work, which is expected to be in proportion to the time spent in prayer.

The orphanages that were funded by following these guidelines were first-class. The furnishings, children's clothing and other supplies, were the best money could buy.[4]

You have heard it so often it probably does not mean anything to you anymore, but it is still true: You cannot outgive God.

The few examples we have used to describe excesses and rip-offs which are found in reputable as well as in gimmick churches are but a small sample of what is happening in our country. We have not even scratched the surface. Most of us feel that what these religious organizations are doing is wrong not only in the eyes of the law but also in the eyes of God. But what about the situation within the Body of Christ, our own church? Maybe we in the church have already met the enemy, and "they are us," as the comic strip character Pogo said.

On the Road to Success

As I travel around the country, holding seminars for groups of pastors and church leaders, I see too many churches that have developed a philosophy that "bigger is better." This thinking has become so prevalent that many pastors are forced—or at least they think they are—into a Glitter Gospel concept. They measure success in how big, how many, how much: How big is a facility? How many people can it seat? How much is the offering?

A generation ago, the mainline denominational church was the "respectable" church to attend. Not much happened in church, but it was the place to be on Sunday morning. Friends and neighbors were all there and we were all expected to sit in for an hour. The little Pentecostal churches, however, were looked upon as "those people" who carried on in a less than respectable manner. They were usually in the poorer section of town, and their members did not dress very well. We looked upon them as fanatics "we don't want to be associated with." However, in the past 20 years a major change has taken place in the churches of America.

God, in His wisdom, brought about this change. His Spirit began to move within many of the "respectable" mainline church folk. At first the results were slight, one here, one there. Perhaps a couple felt dissatisfied with the lack of worship in their church. Or a single lady longed to hear about the Good News of Jesus instead of the social gospel. Maybe one day a mainline pastor began to sense, really sense, the presence of the Lord during his time of meditation and prayer. Even some Roman Catholics felt a desire to hear the full gospel preached.

As these folk experienced the power of the Spirit of God on them they attempted to tell others in their "respectable" churches about their feelings. Most of the time they were met with less than open enthusiasm. In some cases they encountered outright hostility.

What were they to do? They knew that what was happening to them was from God. They knew they could no longer sit in the congregations of "social gospel" churches without bursting from the glory of Jesus. Yet they knew that many of their brothers in Christ would be offended if they did not behave in a "respectable" way. They were forced to sit on their enthusiasm lest they be called "fanatic."

Some did not contain themselves and were asked to leave the church they had grown up in, they were given the left foot of fellowship. Where were they to go? Many found their way to the little Pentecostal churches across town, the church that not long ago they thought of as "those people who do strange things." Here they discovered that they could worship with all the joy they now felt.

Others stayed within their mainline denominations but sneaked off across town for the Sunday evening service of worship and praise. They became, in essence, double agents. As more and more felt the desire to worship with the enthusiasm their spirits longed for, the little church across town began to grow at a faster rate than ever before. As a matter of fact, it was now becoming "respectable."

Growth was so rapid they found they needed more room to accommodate the numbers of people attending services. The "little" church was no longer little; it had grown in size and wealth and was soon more than just respectable, it was acceptable. That was when their problems began. Soon many would learn the price of success.

"Let's Build!"

Even though the offerings and tithes increased as a result of the rapid growth, the church kept pretty much within their small-church budget. They added no new leaders and the pastor was too busy ministering to his growing congregation to take time to get additional training in administration. As he always had, the pastor did pretty much as he wanted to and the church looked to him for complete leadership, both spiritually and in business matters—even though he was not trained to manage an organization the size his church was rapidly becoming.

The pastor had only the example of his fellow pastors to look to for help, those who also were not trained in the areas of accounting, managing large budgets, controlling building programs in excess of millions of dollars, complex tax laws, etc. The congregation expected the pastor to continue in his traditional role as administrator and spiritual leader. Few doubted his role of complete authority over the larger congregation. Those who doubted or had questions did not speak up, or if they did they were told that "the pastor knows best."

Soon it was obvious that a major building program was required. The pastor, in the excitement and glow of success, let his desires get ahead of God. "Look how fast we're growing. Surely, growth will continue. Let's build!" They first located and purchased land to accommodate new facilities the expanded congregation required. "Five acres will do us now, but will it be enough in 10 years?" Plans were needed, "Let's get the best architect we can so that the buildings are at least as nice as those other churches." Church school continued to grow by leaps and bounds and "we need facilities that will accommodate future church school growth." All of this made sense to the congregation, so the little church proceeded to sell its present facility.

It was soon evident that the cost of the new facility had been underestimated—by about half. But the church had gone too far to turn back now, besides, "It's all needed, so we must press on. God will provide."

When the church set about seeking funds to finance their building program they discovered that they did not qualify the way industry does. When industry borrows construction money it can come up with profit and loss statements, records of accounts receivable, a certain amount of inventory and equipment. Most of the time it also has a history of being able to pay back loans.

A church, on the other hand, has little or none of these assets; it has basically the tithes and offerings of the congregation and pledges, on paper, for the building program, not very bankable in the eyes of the lender. Banks and other lending institutions are reticent to lend large amounts to a church that is building a single-purpose building, and bank examiners realize that tithes, offerings and pledges cannot be counted on in the long haul. Also, lenders do not want to be put in a position where foreclosure might be necessary. Not only is it bad for their public relations, it is also hard to recoup their investment from buildings that are designed for one purpose only—as a church.

"Creative Financing"

The church found it could not borrow sufficient funds in the normal way. They must look to creative finance methods. What do we mean by creative finance methods?

The story of another church that began a building program describes what could happen when organizations are forced to seek other than conventional forms of loans for construction.

In the early seventies a church in California began to realize that, because of rapid growth, they would soon need new facilities—at least in the minds of the leadership. They proceeded to make plans to sell their present facilities and begin a building program. They determined that they would need in excess of a million dollars for land and construction. They soon discovered that the costs of conventional loans—points, interest, fees, etc.—were out of line and that a reasonable financing package was not available.

By now the old facility had been sold and the church was in a bind to get some action as soon as possible. They hired a "director of stewardship." His efforts brought to light a situation that looked promising. A church in a nearby city had established a "trust fund" to finance their building project. Further investigation revealed that a number of churches in the district were using the trust-fund concept for construction, expansion, or to buy property. Therefore, the leaders of the church assumed that this method of financing must be acceptable and within the law. They decided that they too would finance construction of the new church through the trust-fund method.

A brochure was prepared spelling out in detail how the trust worked. The church had a document printed that resembled a stock certificate, and an account was opened at a local bank, which became the trust. The leaders did not seek approval from any governmental authority, either because they were not aware they should or because they felt they knew what they were doing.

The pastor announced from the pulpit and in the church newsletter that the church would accept funds into the trust and that interest on these funds would be paid. The interest would be in excess of the current interest paid at banks or savings and loan institutions. It was stated that a reserve larger than that required by a bank or savings and loan would be maintained and that the money could be withdrawn any time.

Some five months after the inception of the trust, the state, through the Corporations Commissioner, notified the church that the Department of Corporations considered the trust fund to be a security. Since the trust fund was considered a security, it was not exempt from registration requirements. The letter from the state was not shown to the congregation or to the many investors.

Money continued to come into the fund, interest was paid, banking records were kept, and the fund was used to finance construction of the new facility. By this time, the cost of the project had increased from the one-million-dollar estimate to more than five million. The congregation and leadership took great pride in the fact that "this church will be one of the largest in the state."

The trust fund continued to grow, and little, if any, attention was paid to the letter stating that the commissioner considered the fund to be a security. The pastor continued to promote the fund from the pulpit and through the, by now, rather extensive newsletter that found its way to interested people in and out of the state. The fund was paying higher interest rates than could be obtained from a bank or savings and loan and was considered a "good deal" by the many investors.

Right or Wrong, We Need It!

Early in the life of the fund, the leaders of the church had met with the representative of the Corporate Commissioner's office. The representative explained that certain requirements must be met: the fund brochure must show how the funds were to be used and if they were for a specific building project; impound of the funds must take place; each investor should be a "knowledgeable investor"; only discretionary dollars could be allowed as investment funds; funds were to be handled through some sort of recision offer; existing depositors should have a full explanation of the involvement of the Corporate Commissioner. A lot to ask and not all of these requirements were followed by the fund administrators.

Prior to starting the new building, the church had sold the property it had occupied for many years. The funds from the sale were initially deposited into the trust fund. Shortly after the Commissioner became involved, and the fund seemed to be heading for potential trouble, the church leaders opted to withdraw the money from the sale of the property. After all, "This was the church's money and couldn't be risked." Little consideration was given to the "risk" of trust fund depositors. The congregation was told that it was necessary to withdraw the funds in order to "reflect proper accounting procedures," which was a stretching of the truth.

Shortly after the church funds were withdrawn, the Department of Corporations issued a letter outlining very stringent new rules regarding the trust. These new rules required that land and construction costs be financed by other than the trust fund and that a full recision offer be made.

A few months later a new and more stringent letter was received saying that the trust funds could not be used at all, and that all funds left in the trust must be administered by a bank or savings and loan and that the administrator should not allow more than 35 percent of the funds to be used for capital improvements. The letter outlined other technical requirements the church would have to meet, many of which would have caused the church to either shut down the fund or lose control of it.

Church leaders decided they could not comply with the requirements. The question of right or wrong was not considered, only whether or not and how long the church leadership could get away with what they were doing. Despite the obvious violations, the trust continued to function for almost four more years. Because of the pressures of increased construction costs and the constant need for more funds, the trust tried to attract more depositors by offering higher and higher interest rates, even though the fund was by now not earning enough to pay the old rate— in fact it was going deeper and deeper in the red.

Finally, approximately six years from the date the fund was started, the state stopped the trust from accepting any more funds. The Department of Banking at last issued a desist order, and the church complied. Many of the investors lost their life savings. Legal battles followed and the church made the headlines throughout the area. And it all started out for the "glory of God."

What a tragic example of getting ahead of God and of poor stewardship. But this church is not unique; this sort of practice is common with those churches that have a "bigger is better" concept of church growth.

It does no good for us to lay guilt on any particular church or ministry. If there is any guilt it belongs to all of us for allowing the Body to be caught in the competitive aspects of the world. Sometimes, the enemy is us!

In chapter 11 are some suggestions—straight from God's Word—which we can all follow in putting our own house in order. If you are a pastor or church leader you might consider these steps for a more reliable, consistent ministry for the glory of God. If you are not a church leader, perhaps your pastor would be willing to listen as you discuss these steps with him or her.

6

The Skeleton Is in Our Own Closet!

Yes, Tom (Dick, Harry), I believe in the power of the gospel (in world missions, that healing is for everyone); therefore, I will pledge to support this ministry with:

$_____ per month

$_____ one-time commitment

_____ prayer support

Sound familiar?

Every day we in America are approached by many organizations asking for support. We receive piles of non-profit mail, all soliciting funds, and hear hours of appeal on radio and television for support of the ministry. Most of these are "emergency needs" of Christian ministries.

If we were to analyze those needs we would discover that a good many of them have come about through deficit

In all too many ministries, gold seems to have become as important as God, and good public relations and clever marketing schemes more widespread than the Good News."

spending; in other words, the debt these ministries have incurred has put them in bondage. Often these organizations are the ones with the biggest buildings, the highest prayer towers, the most modern television studios and the greatest amount of TV or radio air time. Always bigger, and always the most.

Chuck Colson, in a newsletter put out by the ministry he represents, said it best when he said he abhorred "emergency" appeals. He related that while he was in Australia, he was warned about the attitude many Australians have in regard to American evangelists who visited their country: they, the American evangelists, seem more interested in the financial returns than they are in reaching lost souls.

Can you see the smile on the deceiver's face? In all too many ministries, gold seems to have become as important as God, and good public relations and clever marketing schemes more widespread than the Good News.

When does a ministry have enough?

How refreshing it would be to hear a TV minister announce one day, "Partners, our ministry is being blessed, Christ is preached, souls are being saved, saints are being edified. Hallelujah! God provides," rather than a tearful appeal for more money. Most of us will sincerely say, "I don't care about being rich, I just want enough to be comfortable." The trouble is we rationalize, and soon "enough" changes in direct proportion to our income and our desires. In other words, the more we have the more we want.

The Created or the Creator?

Remember Solomon? At the beginning of his rule all he wanted was wisdom and knowledge so that he could lead

God's people. Then he started accumulating horses and gold and silver. Finally, because it was something his father David had wanted, he built a magnificent Temple for God. But notice, his own palace was much larger and more lavish than the house of God. It appears that Solomon was able to rationalize that his great wealth, unsurpassed power, multiple marriages to pagan women, as well as his wisdom and knowledge, were his right because he was doing all in the name of God and for the growth of the kingdom.

Where did Solomon go wrong? At what point did he stop doing God's work and start doing everything for himself? When he received great wealth? No, material wealth of itself is not evil. God created all things, and what God created is not evil. Besides, God told Solomon he would give him wisdom and "riches and honor, so that there will not be any among the kings like you all your days" (1 Kings 3:13).

We must not fear material things, but we must put them in proper perspective. The Bible does not condemn riches, only the love of riches (see 1 Tim. 6:10). God gives us material aspects for our enjoyment. He rewards His children with an abundance of good things. The problem comes when we place the created ahead of the Creator. At that point, the possession becomes an idol and, when we begin to bask in our abundance, our relationship with God cools down. Revelation 3:17 says:

> You say, "I am rich, and have become wealthy, and have need of nothing," and you do not know that you are wretched and miserable and poor and blind and naked.

Then God warns, "Those whom I love, I reprove and

discipline" (v. 19). We lose when we put our wealth above our need for God's leadership.

Many churches and other Christian ministries become proud of what they achieve. Their big buildings and impressive accomplishments become monuments to their own success: "Just look at what we've done." They concentrate on gathering more "things"—so that "God will be glorified."

Much of our time—as much as 50 percent in some churches—is taken up in planning for building programs, approving budgets, determining the pastor's salary, and raising funds for various activities. We talk a lot about drapes and carpeting, the color of the walls, and whether or no we should put a special message center in the nursery. During these planning sessions, which are usually heated discussions, God takes a back seat. Sometimes we forget who is the created and who is the Creator.

Full of Dead Men's Bones

The Christian community tends to blame the "phoney" or "gimmicky" churches for hurting the image of the true church. As we have seen, however, it is not always those religious organizations formed for the purpose of sidestepping the IRS that hurt the image of God's Church. Often the legitimate, hard-working, sincere ministries fall prey to the idea that "bigger is better."

In the last chapter we discussed a church that made wrong decisions. The leadership departed from the truth. They elected to borrow money from the congregation by deceit and they knowingly violated the law. However, lest you think I am singling them out, let me give you a few examples of other situations that have occurred in recent years.

In Ohio, a ministry that included a church raised more

than $12 million through the use of notes which they could not repay. The organization was charged with scheming to defraud the noteholders because it did not disclose its financial condition to the investors.

A minister in Oregon sold investment certificates throughout the country, promising a high rate of interest. At maturity these certificates could not be redeemed because of a lack of funds. The minister was charged with failure to comply with the securities law, misrepresentation, and illegally diverting more than three million dollars to a corporation the ministry owned. More than seven thousand investors faced total loss of the money they had invested in the certificates.

The list of churches that have attempted to raise funds through methods other than what the Bible teaches is long. What is worse, many of these churches and ministries are "lights set on a hill." They had already attracted the attention of those who lived outside their immediate communities because they were doing good work for the Lord; but when they became convinced that "bigger is better" and got mixed up in questionable ways of raising funds, their negative witness reached far wider than their positive ministry had. In every case the leaders of these ministries got ahead of God.

In Colorado a church raised funds through the use of bonds to build a nursing home. Some six years later the nursing home still was not completed and the money was gone. What happened to the funds raised by the bonds? It was used for television and other means of "communicating the gospel." Eventually, the pastor was indicted for fraud and the church filed bankruptcy. Many bond holders were not paid in full for their investments and creditors had to accept pennies on the dollars for their materials and labor.

This effort started out to glorify God; but it ended up just another humiliating witness of the Christian Church to the world.

Here again, however, God has worked in His mysterious way to heal the wounds in this part of His Body. In the March 1987, edition of *Charisma* Magazine, John Sherrill tells how one of the victims of this unsuccessful investment attempt went "the second mile" to help bring about the restoration of funds to those who had invested in the hospital in good faith. By 1974, J. Allan Petersen had become discouraged by the high-pressure campaign this great church was waging to sell bonds for the hospital project. He also was given "a runaround" when he tried to get money back to some of his friends who had invested in the project. As a result he broke off what had been a valuable friendship with the pastor. But twelve years later, in 1986, he began to help his former pastor and friend to pay back $6 million the church still owed to its creditors and investors. He wrote a letter to 800 investors explaining that he was a friend of the pastor who was trying to discover a few facts: How much money was still needed to pay off the debts? Do you want all of your principal returned? Would you consider reducing the amount? Could you forgive the entire sum?

He received replies from three-fourths of the people. When the results were tallied, the amount had been reduced by $2 million. Then Petersen began to call on fellow evangelists and church leaders throughout the country, asking not for donations but for their prayers. These leaders, men like Pat Robertson, Morris Cerullo, Kenneth Hagin, Jim Bakker, Bill Bright, Kenneth Copeland, Tim LaHaye, Ted Engstrom, Jack Hayford, Jerry Falwell, Oral Roberts, and others, as well as pastors of smaller churches around the country, not only prayed, they also began to contribute to the "Second Mile" funds. Today the amount still outstanding is just under $2 million. That's the way the Body should respond to its hurting members![1]

"Remember Therefore from Where You Have Fallen"

A "success syndrome" causes leaders to lose sight of the purpose of the Church. Nowhere in God's Word do we find that success is measured by bigger buildings, bigger cars, or bigger TV audiences. What we do find in God's Word is that we are to be servants, to take care of the widows and orphans, heal the sick (spiritually and physically) and spread the Good News of our Lord and Savior, Jesus Christ. What is the meaning of "success" if the witness of the Church is put in a bad light, whether by naiveté or deliberate ignorance of the law? Who becomes the winner? Only the enemy. Jesus told us to "go therefore and make disciples of all the nations," but I do not think He meant for us to do it through deception or lying. The Lord, in the Apostle John's vision on the island of Patmos, told him to write to one of the churches and say:

> I know your deeds and your toil and persever-
> ance, . . . and you have perseverance and have
> endured for My name's sake, and have not
> grown weary. But I have this against you, that
> you have left your first love. Remember there-
> fore from where you have fallen, and repent and
> do the deeds you did at first; or else I am com-
> ing to you, and will remove your lampstand out
> of its place—unless you repent (Rev. 2:2-5).

Most churches that find themselves in financial hot

We as a Church are in a battle that requires our all-out effort to remain spotless and without blemish."

water such as we have mentioned are Bible believing, Bible preaching centers of worship that desire to bring people to the Lord. Most of them are bright witnesses for God and lead many people into a relationship with Jesus. But, when they choose to go ahead of God financially, not only is their witness to the world in general hurt, new babies in Christ are also hindered from further maturity in the Lord.

We as a Church are in a battle that requires our all-out effort to remain spotless and without blemish. *Time* Magazine, which does not always present Christian ministries in a favorable light, used Billy Graham as an example of financial integrity. In an article, "Enterprising Evangelism," the author comments that decades ago, Billy Graham "pioneered a cleanliness campaign among evangelists by taking a straight salary (currently $59,100 plus housing allowance and expenses) rather than living off unaudited gifts." The article explains that Graham gave control of his ministry to an independent board of businessmen, and began to issue audited financial statements.[2]

Billy Graham still gets the highest TV ratings of any preacher during his prime-time crusades.

John White, in his book *The Golden Cow,* asks:

> But you may be wondering about the church we both love, what of her future? What will happen when freedom falls about our ears here in the West (as surely it will sooner or later)? How will the church survive? Certainly she will not survive in her present outward form. Certainly her whoredoms will be painfully, humiliatingly exposed. Undoubtedly some groups will suffer both unthinkable persecutions and unspeakable glories. God has not changed, nor has the

nature of evil. History is still in some measure repeating itself. The twentieth century need not expect to escape all that has been going on for centuries. It seems rather to be bringing the strands of world history together.

Dark clouds fill the horizon. Perhaps every century has had a sense of the apocalyptic, but the twentieth has more reason to have it than most. We are a global village. We are no longer a vast world but a shrunken spaceship, our lives bound together inexorably by an invisible network of communication. The twentieth century is unique. Humankind can for the first time destroy itself. Our technological powers have reached their zenith while our moral capacity remains as feeble as ever. Our knowledge has never been greater, our wisdom more abysmal.[3]

Where Have All the Wise Men Gone?

The corporate church of Christendom has a major problem. How can it set about cleaning up the present problems and then avoid future problems?

The Word of God tells us to seek wise counsel; pastors can be willing to listen to members of the congregation or to wise counselors who are experienced in such matters as they caution against getting involved in something that may have disastrous consequences.

If a church's leadership does not understand the perimeters of the laws concerning financing and borrowing money, there are many Christian attorneys and businessmen who can advise them. Leaders need to be open and willing to discuss these matters with those who know and not let their own desires for "bigness" cloud their thinking. If we in the church continue to flaunt the law and receive bad publicity for our actions, more and more people are going to agree with what Madaline Murray O'Hair says:

> A trust fund here, a common stock there, corporate loans, there probably is no form of business ownership or investment in which the churches are not involved and from which they do not derive, no one knows how many tens of millions of dollars of tax free income at the tax payers' expense, and until the churches are forced to disclose their holdings, no one will know. The principle on which our nation is founded is that religion is a private affair and not a public one. That therefore it should not be assisted by government at the expense of the general taxpayer. Moreover, other eleemosynary (charitable) organizations unlike the churches are required by law to file yearly information returns with the IRS. They must also report to the FCC, and other regulatory agencies. Organized religion is not placed under any such reporting control.[4]

As it relates to reporting requirements. this well-known atheist is pretty close to right; and she is right in some cases about the first part of her statement.

I read Ms. O'Hair's statement to a class of seminary students, most of whom were deeply involved in church activities, and asked for their comments. I did not tell them who wrote it. Not one student disagreed with the statement. After the class, one young man came to me to discuss a problem he had been having regarding the pastor of the church where he was interning. Not only was the pastor not reporting his earnings to the government, he also was not reporting them to the congregation. Most of the hard cash never got into the church record books, only as far as his pocket. When questioned by the young man the pastor told him to "grow up" and face the fact that what he was doing was common practice for most pastors. Thank God, I could tell the young student that by far the majority of pastors love God more than money and under-the-table salaries were not a common practice.

The tragic part of the above incident is that the pastor saw no wrong in skimming the collections. He is not to be excused for his practice but it is hard to condemn him because he is only reflecting the environment in which he was raised. He had been taught that a pastor is God's man and thus could do no wrong, and the flock must not reproach the pastor under any condition. It is easy to rationalize that "after all, the money is God's and I am God's man at this church."

I also was wrong. I should have gone with the young man and confronted the pastor and his church. I hid my head in the sand and rationalized every bit as much as the skimming pastor did. My rationalization was to let God handle it and "keep out of it."

I believe God was disappointed that I did not deal openly and honestly with the pastor. I should have been more concerned with what Scripture tells us about confronting a brother who is sinning. I am sure the young pastor has been disillusioned by both his pastor and by me. How much better it would have been had I followed God's Word and gone with the young man to the pastor and confronted him in love, offered to pray with him for forgiveness, and stopped a wrong from going any further.

Instead, in all likelihood, the pastor continues to skim to supplement his salary to support his life-style, rationalizing the whole time. His sin affected not only himself, but also the young intern and the members of their church. But what about the wrong committed in the eyes of the IRS?

If the pastor failed to report his skimmed money on his tax return, which is likely, then he is in violation of the tax law and is guilty of tax evasion. Here is another example of not obeying the scriptural admonition to submit to governing authorities.

Suppose we assume that this pastor acted the way he did because of his "rights" under the Constitution? In the next chapter we will look at the history of the separation of church and state, the Constitution, and our rights.

7

Hanky-Panky Under the Covers of Freedom

We hear so much about our right to freedom of religion in our nation. Have you ever read exactly what the Constitution has to say on the subject?

> Congress shall make no law respecting the establishment of religion, or prohibiting the free exercise thereof, or abridging the freedom of speech, or of the press, or the right of the people peaceably to assemble or to petition the government for the redress of grievances.

There you have it, the First Amendment to the Constitution of the United States of America. Less than 50 words and, it would appear, only the first part of it pertains to the church. How can lawyers make a career out of just these few words? How can this short paragraph be so important that the Supreme Court of the land almost always has a case regarding the First Amendment on the docket?

Does Freedom Mean Unrestrained?

Some people wonder if the First Amendment was passed so that government might have authority to restrict the church in its activities. Clifton E. Ohmstead, author of *The History of Religion in the United States,* clarifies this point:

> The purpose of the amendment was not to work hardship upon the Christian church, but rather to discourage rivalry from the various denominations for government favors, and to prevent any national establishments whether of denominational or interdenominational character. The effect of the amendment was not to protect Americans from religion but to insure the vitality and strengthening of religion. The experience of its framers was that the state support can further complacency and thus render the denominations' efforts ineffectual.[1]

Ohmstead is explaining that the framers of the amendment were being pushed by Baptists, Presbyterians, Quakers, and Jeffersonian Deists for separation from state controls. Their churches had not been free but were under government control and they wanted to be sure this newly formed country had rules to protect them from control in the future.

James Madison summed up their sentiments in a memorial to Congress in which he echoed the conviction a cleric made more than two hundred years before:

> Religion or the duty which we owe to our crea-

tor and the manner of discharging it can be directed only by reason and conviction. Not by force or violence. The religion then of everyone must be left to the conviction and conscience of every man. It is the right of every man to exercise it as these may dictate. The right is in his nature and an inalienable right.[2]

When the pilgrims came to this country, primarily to find freedom to worship as they saw fit, they established colonies in Plymouth and Boston and began to teach the views of John Calvin: Government was established for the sole purpose of curbing sin and was ordained by God. There was no thought given to human equality; the church state was ruled by the elect. The purpose was not toleration but the establishment of a secure religion. There is not much religious freedom in this viewpoint; however, at that time and in that place, this attitude was necessary for people who had fled state controlled churches.

Over a period or years and through many problems, including the Toleration Act of 1649, religious freedom became a fact within the 13 original colonies. There was a diversity of views, yet a Christian base was overwhelmingly predominant.

In 1787 the Constitutional Convention faced a problem: How to find a common denominator among the various attitudes that ranged from the establishment of religion to total religious freedom. It is interesting to note that the Constitution was ratified on September 17, 1787, but the First Amendment was not ratified until December 15, 1791. Why did the framers wait four years to draft the First Amendment?

The framers of the Constitution had differing views in many areas, and particularly in relationship to church and state. Alexander Hamilton was for a Christian society that supported both the church and the state. Other founding fathers thought that, because of the past history of the church dominating the state and the state dominating the church, America must not permit an alliance between church and state. They were as much concerned with freedom from religion as they were with freedom of religion. The doubts and confusion that delayed the decision concerning church and state for more than four years was not that the government might control the church, but rather that the church might control the government.

The key point regarding religion was that Congress could not enact any law that would establish a state or national church, such as existed in Germany and England following the reformation. However, Jefferson and Madison were equally concerned with the rights of the individual in regard to religious liberty. Because of that concern the First Amendment included restrictions against Congress passing any law that would prohibit the free exercise of religion.

If the 1787 Constitution had included the wording and intent of the First Amendment, it is doubtful that it would have been ratified. It took four years for the First Amendment to become law.

"Congress Shall Make No Law . . . "

The First Amendment contains no specific reference to the separation of church and state. However, a study of historical documents indicates that the founders clearly intended that separation was the intent of the amendment.

Elwin A. Smith explains:

The republican philosophy was strictly separa-

We cannot have our cake and eat it too.
We cannot on one hand ask for
separation and on the other hand seek
financial or other assistance or exclusion."

---

tionist. Not only out of respect for individual right but also lest any measurable restoration of the church state alliance prompt a return to the aristocratic social order. The church must remain under the sole control of their own adherents, and be supported exclusively by them.[3]

It would seem that the statement, "Congress shall make no law respecting the establishment of religion," is the basis for separation of church and state. If our churches are to retain our rights within this statement we must not only resist government infringement but also refuse government support.

We cannot have our cake and eat it too. We cannot on one hand ask for separation and on the other hand seek financial or other assistance or exclusion.

Supreme Court Justice Black has defined the establishment clause in this way:

The Establishment of religion clause of the first amendment means at least this, neither the state nor the federal government can set up a church, neither can it pass laws which aid one religion, aid all religions, but prefers one religion over another. Neither can it force or influence a person to go or remain away from a church against his will or force him to profess a belief or disbelief of any religion. No tax in any amount large or small can be levied to support any religious activities or institutions, whatever they may be called or whatever form they may adopt to teach or practice religion.[4]

The Constitution guarantee of free exercise means that each person is free to profess whatever faith he chooses, or no faith at all, without government interference. To broaden its meaning so that one religion would benefit over others is a potential threat to this freedom we Christians love and hold dear.

The right of an individual to choose does not, however, give him the right to do as he will concerning government. He may accept religion or he may reject it, but he may not reject the laws concerning that part which government must play in the establishment and protection of churches without becoming liable to punishment. This may sound as though I am taking sides with the government and against the church. I am not doing so.

I believe the Constitution gives us the right to choose our religion as long as we do not impose our choice on other members of society. The Constitution does not give us the right to violate the law of the land, and as Christians we are not free to violate the law as long as the law does not contradict God's Word.

The government, even with its weaknesses, is vital to the church and to Christians. Martin Luther was persecuted greatly by government in his time; however, instead of finding fault in government and demanding his rights, he wrote:

> It [the government] is a glorious, divine ordinance and an excellent gift of God, who has established it, and wants to have it maintained. Government is certainly something that man cannot do without. If there were none, no one could live because of other men. One would devour the other, as brute beasts do to one another. Do you think that if a bird or a beast

could speak and see government among
humans, they wouldn't say, "Oh, you dear people, you are not men, you are gods compared to
us. How safe you sit, live, and have everything
while we are never safe from one another for an
hour as to life, shelter, or food. Woe to your
unthankfulness."⁵

· We need to consider Luther's words and be thankful
for a government-established system of justice and order.
The government's job is concerned with the world, and
we live in the world. The job of the church is to call people
away from the evil aspects of the world and to bring them
to a saving knowledge of Jesus Christ and to prepare them
not only for eternal life, but also to give a good witness
here on earth. The government, in the scheme of things,
should provide the church the protection afforded by the
Constitution so that the church can develop the type of cit-
izen that obeys the laws established by a good government.

The government must not limit the freedom of the
church and the church must not abuse the freedom
afforded it. The time has come—and I pray that it is not
too late—for church leaders and lay people to take the
glitter out of the gospel and get back to the Great Commission. We are to be to the world "an example of those
who believe" (1 Tim. 4:12). We need to go the extra mile
in setting an example of submitting to authority.

What if going that extra mile begins to limit our Constitutional right of free worship?

The Red Tape Jungle

Lately, many churches have accused the government of

church abuse because authorities now require more reporting forms than ever before and are entangling the churches in more red tape. Of course, as we have discussed, the reason for this "abuse" is that there are many "churches" which have been organized for the purpose of tax evasion and Christian churches that play games to avoid taxation. The situation is so bad that many people are concerned that we will lose our tax exempt status.

We do still have tax exemption, as well as other government considerations, and we should continue to fight for these rights so that we do not lose them. For example, consider the rights of the Amish in relation to public schooling, or the rights of the Seventh-day Adventists to still receive employment benefits if they opt not to work on Saturdays. Without such privileges the government would no longer be separated from the affairs of the church. However, there are still those who abuse these rights.

The traditional church of the Lord Jesus Christ needs to face the challenge and become aware of the historical aspects of the First Amendment and all legislation that has evolved from this amendment. Church leaders must learn the laws, the reasons behind the laws, and vow to uphold them in administering the financial affairs of our churches.

When we have done our homework, then we need to sit down with various government agencies and work out the differences we find in how we each interpret the First Amendment. The Church of God is not a building or a denomination, but is the Body of Christ, people who follow Christ. The Church cannot be put into a neat little box and told what the government thinks we should do. The Church must be a dynamic force, functioning in a viable way throughout society. We do not always meet in grand buildings; some of us meet in homes or in storefronts. We

The best defense the Church can make is to be an impeccable witness for our Lord, and to stop abusing the privileges that are ours under the First Amendment."

are from all walks of life and do not always fit the image the world has of what a church "should be." We need to help Congress to define more accurately what a church is without dissecting the church.

It is understandable that Congress has not been able to see the Church as the Body of Christ. We do not always act like members of a Body. We amputate ourselves from the Body. We build walls and dare the government to knock them down, all the while demanding our First Amendment rights.

Before the Church can help Congress define the term *church*, we need to more clearly define what we think we are as a church. Then governing authorities will have some guidelines to determine what a church is and to delineate which organizations can legally be protected by the First Amendment.

The Treasury Department is not out to shut down the church, any church; but they will be working to eliminate the religious tax exempt status abuser, the cheater and the fraud. If they are forced to do this without proper input from the Church, it will be our own fault. Remember, we are not only the Church, we are also the government, and both areas require our involvement.

The best defense the Church can make is to be an impeccable witness for our Lord, and to stop abusing the privileges that are ours under the First Amendment. We need to set our priorities straight. We should be concerned for people, not for material wealth. God will provide the means to further His ministry without our having to break the laws of our land and His commandments.

> Act as free men, and do not use your freedom
> as a covering for evil, but use it as bondslaves
> of God (1 Pet. 2:16).

8

Where Is Little Boy Blue?

One theme heard frequently from television evangelists is that of prosperity. Many Christians, with tongue in cheek, refer to these messages as "prosperity gospel." Those who grab hold of these messages cling to every verse in the Bible that seems to promise them material wealth. They listen to the formulas guaranteeing to make them prosperous: "If you do this, then God will do this; after all, does God lie?"

It would seem, from listening to these messages, that the promise of wealth is as critical to the Christian—or at least to the Christian leader—as is the promise of eternal life.

God did promise to make His people prosper if they obeyed His Word. Jesus did say that all our needs will be met "according to His riches in glory in Christ Jesus" (Phil. 4:19). And Satan has heard all this and has been using money as one of his most effective tools for the destruction of God's people.

Even the arrest, trial and crucifixion of Jesus was triggered by the love of money. Two of the religious leaders in Jerusalem—the high priest, Caiaphas, and his father-in-law, the ex-high priest, Annas—risked their positions in order to bring Jesus to His death. They were eager to violate most of the laws of the Hebrew court regarding the conducting of a trial in order to stop Jesus. What caused them to be so angry at Jesus?

Annas was high priest for seven years before being forced by the Roman procurator to step down because he was imposing too many capital sentences. He appointed his son-in-law Caiaphas as high priest. During the time he was high priest, Annas firmly established himself and his family as the sole operators of the booths in the Court of the Gentiles of the Temple. He still had this profitable monopoly when Jesus cleansed the Temple of the money-changers. Jesus, by His actions, became a threat to Annas's family's finances as well as to his personal prestige. Their fear of Jesus' power triggered a rage in Annas and Caiaphas that exceeded their fear of God.[1]

"Shepherds Feeding Themselves!"

Satan had been using the love of money to trip up God's spiritual leaders for centuries before Jesus was brought to trial. In the Old Testament the love of the "good life" was often the cause of sin in those who were supposed to shepherd God's flock. In chapter one we saw that Ezekiel was a "watchman" for God who was told to warn God's shepherds about their sin:

> Then the word of the Lord came to me saying,
> "Son of man, prophesy against the shepherds of

Some of God's shepherds still expect
the sheep to provide them with the good life."

Israel. Prophesy and say to those shepherds,
'Thus says the Lord God, "Woe, shepherds of
Israel who have been feeding themselves!
Should not the shepherds feed the flock? You
eat the fat and clothe yourselves with the wool,
you slaughter the fat sheep without feeding the
flock""" (34:1-3).

As we have discovered in the previous chapters, nothing has changed. Some of God's shepherds still expect the
sheep to provide them with the good life. Yes, these shepherds provide some food to the flock, but much of it is
cake, not body building nourishment. They preach messages that tickle the ears of the sheep and cause goose
bumps of excitement. But sheep cannot thrive and grow
on goose bumps.

Sheep need a shepherd who will lead them to food and
water, who will put them first and his own desires second,
and who will, if need be, even die for them.

History bears out that spiritual leaders in every age
have been guilty of putting their love of money before their
concern for the people they are commissioned to lead.
Prior to the Reformation the church held tremendous
political clout, and Rome became the seat of this political
power. The church had become a tool which various
power factors in Europe employed for their own use, and
the pope was the center of the power. Each pope tried to
surpass his predecessor in glory. In an effort to raise
money to pay for the excesses in their offices, the popes
started to issue indulgences.

Indulgences, in theory, allowed the saints to pay for
their sins by contributing to the treasury of the church,
thereby spending less time in purgatory. Indulgences
became such an important part of the treasury of the Vati-

can that they were soon extended to include those souls already in purgatory.

A young scholar and priest, Martin Luther, began to question the validity of indulgences when the pope, in a fund-raising program, stated that indulgences should be extended to still another group. The seminary at which Luther was a professor housed a famous collection of relics. The pope decided that those who viewed the collection should be granted indulgences also, provided they made the required contribution. The pope's "financial promoter," a Dominican named Tetzel, went so far as to claim that "as soon as money in the coffer rings, another soul from purgatory springs."

At this point, Luther openly challenged indulgences and declared that the pope had no power to release souls from purgatory. His open defiance brought about the debates that led to the Reformation.[2]

The pope in his desire for more and more money to build bigger and greater monuments is very similar to today's church leader who strives to be greater than his contemporary. And, like the pope, today's leader rationalizes that what he is doing is for the glory of God. Do we honestly think that the Great Creator of heaven and earth really needs multimillion dollar buildings?

Are the shepherds of today who feel they need bigger churches, more expensive cars, designer suits, first-class jet travel to meetings and television appearances, gold and diamond jewelry, any different from the shepherds God rebuked in Ezekiel? Or are they any less mistaken than the pre-Reformation pope? I think not.

"Where Is the Boy Who Looks After the Sheep?"

In our desire to witness for Jesus we have become marketers of Jesus. Magazines, aimed at pastors, include ads for sermon ghost writers and for ways to make "huge" profits selling pot holders, leather bound Bibles and the Bible on tape.

Preachers on TV and radio spend much of their time talking about mailing lists. If we get on one mailing list, we are soon on the list of every TV evangelist and magazine publisher in the nation. And, judging from the mail we receive, most of them went to the same school of under- lining. Can Christianity be hawked? Do we need Madison Avenue tricks to "sell" Jesus?

The Apostle Paul spoke of this problem. He was con- cerned about first-century hucksters who were making a profit while corrupting the Word of God:

> For we are not like many, peddling the word of God, but as from sincerity, but as from God, we speak in Christ in the sight of God (2 Cor. 2:17).

God continues to strive with religious leaders who "peddle" the Word of God for a price. But He will not let them get away with dishonoring His name forever.

What finally happened with the shepherds, the priests of Israel, that Ezekiel spoke about?

> Therefore, you shepherds, hear the word of the Lord: "Thus says the Lord God, 'Behold, I am against the shepherds, and I shall demand My sheep from them and make them cease from feeding sheep. So the shepherds will not feed themselves any more, but I shall deliver My flock from their mouth, that they may not be food for them'" (Ezek. 34:9-10).

Modern-day shepherds, learn from the lesson in Ezekiel. The churches of today will not profit long if you continue to use the hard-sell methods of Madison Avenue to reach a world that is dying.

He's Heard on the Airwaves Blowing His Horn

What then? Is there no place in radio, TV and other media for the gospel? Of course there is. God has certainly provided these vehicles for His use, so we cannot ignore them. Every tool must be used to reach the lost, but it must be used with wisdom. Without the *Pax Romana* (the peace of Rome) and the roads the Romans built, Paul would not have been able to start the churches or preach to the numbers of people he did. Paul used whatever was available to him to spread the gospel. We must also take advantage of that which God has given us. However, the message we send through the media should be the pure gospel, not the message of "send your tithes and offerings."

Spreading the Good News of Jesus through the airwaves costs a lot of money, and the price is justified because we reach many more people than we could hope to reach any other way. The sin comes when we get ahead of God, when we use what people send in to build ourselves up or make a name for ourselves.

What does it profit the Lord if nine or ten evangelists air at the same time on Sunday morning, all competing for the viewing audience? What value is preaching or teaching if one-third of the time is used to beg for money? What kind of a witness do we present to the world that is watching a TV evangelist or listening to a radio preacher who uses the bulk of his time either appealing for money or boasting about how big or great his ministry is?

Not long ago I received a newsletter from a prominent

evangelist who talked at great length about himself, mentioning his name 17 times on the first two pages and the name of our Savior twice. The bulk of the last page was made up of a picture of the evangelist and a personal appeal telling me how I could invest my money through an annuity, naming his ministry as beneficiary, of course.

Most of us, if we have ever been put on the mailing list of any religious organization, receive this kind of propaganda every day. But what if you were not a believer or were a new Christian who somehow received this kind of communication? Would you be inclined to investigate the plan of salvation? I can tell you from personal experience that the first 40 years of my life were dedicated to running from this sort of thing. I was convinced that very few churches were out for anything from me other than my money. I wonder how many people turn Jesus off each year because of the greed and ego of some of the media "shepherds."

The hurting world needs to hear the simple gospel of Jesus Christ, not hype about how great a ministry is, or how big a church, or how much is needed to keep the ministry on the air, or that they can receive a nightlight in the shape of a cross for sending in a "love gift."

Would it be out of line to ask for time out from radio and TV spending so that leading media personalities could sit down and try to find a way to utilize more effectively the vast sums of money they collectively spend? They all say their primary purpose is to reach the unsaved, thus it should not make any difference who reaches them.

I realize there are several barriers to this suggestion. One barrier is that large amounts of money have been invested by each of these TV ministries in equipment and facilities. So much so that unless the ministries bring in enormous donations each day their bills cannot be paid.

Most of these ministries are in a position of deficit spending, they owe far more than they can bring in. They are forced to spend money hiring marketing specialists to help them find new ways to raise funds. Then they need to hire people to run the computers that keep up with, and increase the number of, names on their mailing lists so that you can get personalized mailings asking you for more money to keep the ministries going. The computer knows you a lot better than the evangelist does. As deficit spending increases, the quality of the ministry decreases because so much effort is put into fund raising.

A Hireling or a Shepherd?

The original intent of each of these ministries, no doubt, was to spread the gospel a little differently than anyone else was doing and to present Christ in a quality way. At first the leaders stayed close to God so they could listen to His instructions. They were good and faithful stewards of the money all the little people sent them. Soon, however, they found they could do a better job with more sophisticated equipment, which, of course, required a building to house the equipment. Then to keep up the image it was necessary to make a "star" out of the ministry's leader, someone the people could identify with. Naturally, a star should be treated like a star. He needed to be flown first class from place to place, or better yet, fly in his own plane. Since he is now the equal to an executive of a large corporation, he should receive a salary worthy of his time.

One day the bookkeeper notices that the costs of the ministry are now exceeding the income. Never mind, God will provide! But instead of waiting for God to provide, the leadership begins to seek out new sources of income on their own. And the hype begins.

God blessed their ministry in the beginning and He would like to continue blessing them, but once they started down their own path, God could no longer lead them. They got puffed up by their own importance, believing the solution was to get bigger and better than the other fellow so they could steal away some of his viewers. The problem was, the other fellow was doing the same thing.

When things started to go wrong the "star" found it hard to seek out or listen to wise counsel from either God or man. His role as leader of a Glitter-Gospel ministry became more important than the role of the Holy Spirit. When a man becomes so important in his own eyes that he hears only what he wants to hear, the next step for him to take is to get rid of the killjoys who want to throw cold water on the "star's" ideas.

This scenario does not sound like the kind of shepherds God wants for His flocks. Pastors and evangelists are called to shepherd and lead people to Christ; they are out of their element when they take on the roles of media experts, superstars, or fund raisers. As Peter says in his first Epistle:

> I exhort the elders among you, as your fellow-elder and witness of the sufferings of Christ, and a partaker also of the glory that is to be revealed, shepherd the flock of God among you, not under compulsion, but voluntarily, according to the will of God; and not for sordid gain, but with eagerness; not yet as lording it over those allotted to your charge, but proving to be examples to the flock (1 Pet. 5:1-3).

Do media superstars consider themselves shepherds? If so, do they do it for "sordid gain"? Many TV evangelists

Stewardship in the Bible was not synonymous with giving; . . . stewardship means management! The Lord has called us all to be stewards of what He has provided."

forget that every $100 dollars they receive in tithes represents $1,000 of someone's salary and, for most donors, a lot of hours of work to earn it. Media people should be better stewards of the people's money. How many "world centers" do we need? Why must we have the most elaborate complexes and cathedrals?

All too often, donations are spent in less than prudent ways, generally not in the way God would have them spent. When the ministry gets deeper and deeper in debt, the leaders cannot understand why God is apparently no longer blessing them.

Stewardship in the Bible was not synonymous with giving; rather, stewardship means management! The Lord has called us all to be stewards of what He has provided. Being constantly in debt and paying high interest rates is not good management. Paying our bills late or rationalizing a way out of paying them at all is not good management. If the truth were known, we would find that the constant seeking of funds is in direct proportion to the demands of our creditors; this in spite of God's warning against getting in debt.

We are always so eager to accept the promises of God that make us feel good, but seldom talk or hear about the warnings that take away our fun. We want to run our lives our way.

9

We Did It Our Way

Behold, the Holy Spirit called all the great men of the Television Church together for a strategy conference. The Reverend Robert Schuller, the Reverend Billy Graham, the Reverend Pat Robertson, the Reverend Oral Roberts, the Reverend Jimmy Swaggert, the Reverend Jerry Falwell, and many others gathered around the large conference table, awaiting the arrival of the Holy Spirit.

And very soon the door opened and the Spirit of Truth took His place at the head of the table. He announced the reason for the conference: "We are here to discuss the problems we seem to be having in reaching the world with the message of Jesus Christ."

Then the Holy Spirit reviewed the works of those in the meeting, and for the most part He was pleased. He often commented, "Well done, good and faithful servant." Soon the tone of the meeting changed as the Leader addressed each man individually and said: "Do I need to remind you that the Crystal Cathedral is mine? Have you forgotten that I am still in charge of O.R.U.? I am still the One who owns the Cathedral of Tomorrow," and such as this, mentioning all the wonderful facilities toward which members of the Body had contributed.

Going around the room He then asked for, and received from each spiritual leader, copies of each ministry's financial statement. He noted that some of the statements indicated that there was money still in reserve; these leaders had been good and faithful stewards of what the Father had put in their charge.

Then He noticed those ministries that were deep in debt, that had been overspending for a very long time. He said, quietly, "Did I tell you to build this lavish apartment? Did I authorize you to use the tithes and offerings for this expenditure? Don't you remember what the Word of God says about going in debt?"

As the tension built, the Holy Spirit held up all the financial statements and asked, "Who does all this belong to?" The immediate response was a hearty, "It belongs to the Lord," but some of those great leaders said it with red faces and downcast eyes. Then the Spirit reminded them that being good stewards of what belongs to God is more important than vanity, ego, and self-aggrandizement as God's servants.

He then told all of them to rise and join hands and repeat after Him: "The Body is not one member, but many. God has placed each member in the Body just as He desired, and there should be no division. Each of us will be concerned for all the other members of the Body. If one member suffers, all members suffer with it; if one member is honored, all members rejoice with it. Above all else we will remember that the Head of the Body is Christ, our Savior and Lord."

Then the Holy Spirit said, "From now on all debts will

be settled, all competition will cease, and each of you will assist the other in all of God's ministries."

The Holy Spirit dismissed the meeting and each of these leaders went back to their ministries determined to give leadership to the Church as a whole. And the Body drew together and paid all their debts and began to seek out God's leadership in all things. And it was never again necessary to beg the people for money, for they were all of one mind to further the Kingdom of God.

A parable? Yes, but can you visualize what would happen within the Body of Christ if such a thing took place? The power that could be generated from these accumulated minds which God could use for His glory, seeing one vision with no self-aggrandizement? the power of the financial resources of the Body all directed toward the Great Commission, united in one operation?

They Did It the Right Way

Up to this point in the book you could very well get the idea that every church and ministry is having trouble keeping afloat. That, of course, is not true. Let me tell you of one church that truly sought God's timing and waited for His answer.

The church was spiritually healthy; the desire of the leadership was simple—hear God and do His will. The fellowship had grown to where the existing facility could no longer accommodate the numbers who attended the Sunday morning worship service and Sunday School. There was more land surrounding the current buildings for expansion, so the church leaders hired an architect to draw plans for a new building that was estimated in excess of half a million dollars to build.

The elders and congregation went to the Lord for guidance. After much prayer they felt free to proceed with the building program. They realized that they would need a new loan and that the loan payment would stretch the current church budget to the limit.

At this point I was called in by the pastor to look at the situation *before* he committed the church to the program. He felt a check in his spirit and decided that an outside opinion was necessary. I studied the feasibility of both their budget and fund raising possibilities. Upon analyzing their records and financial status it became obvious that the fellowship could barely meet the demands of a new loan, and only if all the pledges the congregation had already made were carried through.

Further probing, however, brought to light a fact which they had not considered. The church had purchased the property several years before from an organization that agreed to take a note that included a large balloon payment due after a number of years of relatively small monthly payments. I discovered that the balloon payment was due in two years, and no fund or method of debt retirement had been initiated to meet that balloon payment.

If the pastor, after praying to God for guidance, had ignored the check in his spirit and had gone ahead full blast into a major building program, the church in all probability would not have been able to meet the balloon payment. Upon default the note holder would then have a legal right to initiate foreclosure. The church would have lost the property with its new building, its witness for the Lord to the community at large, the noteholder would have suffered, and the whole mess would have been a disaster to the congregation.

The facilities were needed, but it was not God's timing to go into a major building program before the note was paid for. They stopped the building program with its compounding of debt and went instead into a remodeling program on a pay-as-you-go basis. Then they set in motion a debt-retirement plan to handle the balloon payment.

God honored the integrity of the pastor and the congregation. They have since met the note obligation and find that the remodeled facility is still adequate. At this time they have no debt and the amount they were paying on the mortgage is now being used for missionary work in India.

Seek God and wait for His answer.

Check your timing.

Seek counsel from an outside source or from someone in your congregation who is experienced in the subject.

Do not allow your desires to get ahead of God. Growth is never more important than your witness.

God does not measure success by how big the building is or how many the sanctuary will seat. Neither does He measure success by the size of the mailing list nor the amount in the offering. God does measure success by our obedience to Him and His Word. He looks at our witness to the world and at our faithfulness in the ministry He has put in our charge. He sees how we build up the Body. He tells us to seek counsel from those who are wise in matters at hand.

Attaining to the Unity of the Faith

God's people have now formed several organizations we can utilize to keep us on the right track. If we are a true Church of the Lord Jesus Christ, and are concerned that we keep our ministries in the center of His will, we will seek out the help of some of these organizations.

The CMMA, Christian Ministries Management Asso-

Before we enter into building programs or TV ministries, let us be sure we are following God's leading, not that of our own ego desires."

ciation; Christian Legal Society; EFCA (Evangelical Council for Financial Accountability); and World Vision's long established Christian Leadership Letter are a few of the tools we can use to keep God's leaders and God's Church "pure and unblemished." (See Appendices.)

As good as these organizations are, they still depend on the efforts of each ministry to utilize them. We have the tools, the talents, the resources, and best of all, the power of the Counselor-Comforter-Holy Spirit to get out of debt and get on with winning the world for Christ.

Before we enter into building programs or TV ministries, let us be sure we are following God's leading, not that of our own ego desires. Let us be sure that the timing is right and we are not getting ahead of God. Let us be sure that we have the money *before* we begin the project so that we do not have to go in debt.

The Parable of the Manual of Operation

Business people in the secular world often seek counsel from people who are more knowledgeable in a given area than the business leaders are. When Fred Smith decided to start an overnight delivery service, he hired a management consultant; when Mitch McConnell ran for public office, he hired a political advisor; when the Stouffer Corporation developed a line of diet TV dinners, they hired a package design expert. Today, Smith runs the Federal Express Company, McConnell is a U.S. Senator from Kentucky, and Stouffer's Lean Cuisine is the company's largest selling brand. They all did it with the help of consultants.

At any given moment an estimated 95 percent of Fortune 1,000 industrial corporations, as well as tens of millions of individual Americans, are using consultants.[1]

These professional consultants will not give advice that will tickle the ears of those who hire them; they tell it like it is and give the best advice they are able to give through the wisdom of years of experience.

Counselors are available for the business aspect of the Christian world also. But all too often pastors and other ministry leaders want someone to confirm what they want to do, not someone telling them the wisest way to go.

Of course, there is always the possibility that a professional counselor could give wrong advice. How does a leader in a Christian ministry check out the counselor and his or her advice? Only through God's Word, the Bible. Let us approach this through another parable.

The leaders of growing ministry felt they needed some counsel about a major project they wanted to begin that would cost a lot of money and involve a lot of people. They knew that the Manual of Operation for God's Church, the Bible, says that "a wise man is he who listens to counsel" (Prov. 12:15). The manual told them about when Moses listened to the wise counsel of his father-in-law (Exod. 13-23). So they looked farther in the manual to see what kind of counsel they needed.

First they discovered that the Chief Executive Officer of the Church was not impressed by how high a salary a consultant demanded or what his status was in the community. The Chief Executive Officer wants all the credit for accomplishments in His corporation, and those who seek high salaries and impressive positions often are filled with pride, and "when pride comes, then comes dishonor, but with the humble is wisdom" (Prov. 11:2). So the consultant must be humble.

Next the leaders found that the ministry may need more than one counselor. The Manual of Operation said that "in the abundance of counselors there is victory"

(Prov. 11:14). So they prayed to the Corporate Leader and began to look for the right counselor to guide them in the right way to go. Soon they found a wise and understanding person who gave them good advice. They listened, obeyed, and now are doing a great work for the Kingdom of God.

Hear the Words of the Wise

In the world of secular business, good top level executives are very hard to come by. Executive talent agencies search the country, recruiting men of proven executive ability. A very small percentage of the work force ever becomes truly qualified to be top level management.

In Christian ministries, this very small percentage is reduced even further. Secular business does not require that an executive be born again or even have to believe in a Supreme Being. In Christian leadership, however, we demand that not only must the "executive" be born again, he or she must also believe the same way the top man in the ministry does. If the organization is of the Pentecostal persuasion, all the leaders in the church must be of the same mind. If Lutheran, all must be Lutheran, and so on. A Southern Baptist organization is not inclined to heed the advice of Catholics; an Assembly of God will not seek advice from the Lutherans.

This mind-set results in two problems. The first is that good men who are called of God and have outstanding gifts are not being utilized by the whole Body. The second problem is one the whole Church faces: The practice of placing friends and relatives in leadership positions just because they agree with the philosophy of the man at the top. In many cases the person hired is not the best for the job, but because he is close to the leader and will not make

Leaders of great ministries can become greater by listening to the wise counsel of people who are experts in specific fields."

waves he is put in leadership position. So the whole organization settles for mediocrity and the ministry suffers. Over a period of years the organization will begin to flounder for lack of new concepts and proper management.

When Solomon was starting the giant task of building the Temple he knew that the Hebrews lacked some of the skills he would need to get the job done. Rather than accepting second best, Solomon called on Hiram, king of Tyre for counsel. Hiram wrote back to Solomon and said:

> I am sending a skilled man, endowed with understanding, Huram-abi, the son of a Danite woman and a Tyrian father, who knows how to work in gold, silver, bronze, iron, stone and wood, and in purple, violet, linen and crimson fabrics, and who knows how to make all kinds of engravings and to execute any design which may be assigned to him, to work with your skilled men (2 Chron. 2:13-14).

I am not so sure that Huram-abi was in complete spiritual agreement with Solomon, but he was the best man for the job at hand. Solomon looked for this quality of men to advise him at every step of the Temple construction. The Temple would not have been so magnificent if he had demanded that the skilled advisors be in agreement with him 100 percent, or if he felt his wisdom, great as it was, extended in the area of Temple building.

Leaders of great ministries can become greater by listening to the wise counsel of people who are experts in specific fields. One of the saddest verses in the Bible tells how the mighty kingdom of Israel began to fail. When Rehoboam became king after his father, Solomon, died, he sought out the counsel of the elders who had served his father. They gave the king good advice, derived from their closeness to God and from years of experience. Then the Scriptures tell us:

> But he [Rehoboam] forsook the counsel of the elders which they had given him, and consulted with the young men who grew up with him and served him (1 Kings 12:8).

This decision to follow his friends' advice was the beginning of the end for Rehoboam. The mighty kingdom of David and Solomon was soon divided, with Rehoboam ruling only Judah. In the fifth year of Rehoboam's reign the Egyptians attacked Jerusalem and carried off the treasures of the Temple, the treasures of the king's house, "even . . . all the shields of gold which Solomon had made" (1 Kings 14:26).

How important it is to listen to the "excellent things of counsels and knowledge."

10

Not Borrow! Is God Kidding?

Charge! The sound of that call used to bring to mind a smartly uniformed cavalry unit, bearing down on half-naked Indians with painted faces who were riding hard to meet the soldiers; all of them, Indians and cavalry, shouting and waving rifles in the air.

No more. Now, "Charge!" has to do with smartly dressed—or not-so-smartly dressed—men and women waving small squares of plastic at store clerks, hotel managers, restaurant hostesses, airline desks, and service station attendants.

We live in a buy-now, pay-later generation. Well-meaning, normally sane people from all walks of life follow a pied piper named Madison Avenue into a river of debt; sometimes they get in so deep it takes years to climb out on dry land. This buy-now, pay-later syndrome is another snare from the devil himself. It seems that life will not be worth living unless we can get ahead of, or at least keep up with, the Joneses. We no longer are satisfied with just our "needs," we want all the trimmings and gingerbread surrounding the needs—bigger, faster, more luxuriant autos; more versatile, "energy and water saving" appliances; exotic vacations to faraway places; all on the "easy monthly payment plan." We can even take a trip to the Holy Land and "walk where Jesus walked" on credit, so say many Christian magazines.

Bookstores are filled with books telling us how to "borrow and grow rich"; how to find "ready sources" of money; how to become a "millionaire."

What we seldom read about, however, is the pain and heartache of debt. Madison Avenue does not tell about the day when all the debts must be paid and there is no money to pay them. All they tell you is how to consolidate your debts so that you no longer have a dozen "small" payments, each one with a different rate of interest, but only one monthly payment that is stretched out to last until your children graduate from college. That way, they say, you can have money left over each month for other things you "need." Neither do the ads tell about broken marriages, suicides, alcohol and drug addiction caused by debt.

God's Word, however, does tell us about all this. But just what does God's Word have to say about our "*Charge generation*"?

"*Slaves to the Lender*"

When Joshua led the Israelites over the Jordan River into the Promised Land, God gave him a command:

> This book of the law shall not depart from your mouth, but you shall meditate on it day and night, so that you may be careful to do accord-

ing to all that is written in it; for then you will make your way prosperous, and then you will have success (Josh. 1:8)

The part of God's Word we know that Joshua had were the five books of law which Moses wrote. And one of those books was "Deuteronomy." Deuteronomy has some very definite ideas about how we are to step out in faith and about borrowing money.

> However, there shall be no poor among you, since the LORD will surely bless you in the land which the LORD your God is giving you as an inheritance to possess [many preachers stop at this point], if only you listen obediently to the voice of the LORD your God, to carefully observe all this commandment which I am commanding you today. For the LORD your God shall bless you as He has promised you, and you will lend to many nations, *but you will not borrow;* and you will rule over many nations, but they will not rule over you (Deut. 15:4-6, itals. added).

When God said to "carefully observe all this *commandment,*" He was not just making a recommendation. Why should He be so adamant about borrowing and avoiding debt? The last sentence is the clue. God wants to rule over His people and He knows that the borrower is a slave of the lender, not of God. Solomon echoed this when he wrote: "The rich rules over the poor, and the borrower becomes the lender's slave" (Prov. 22:7). It seems that many of us are willing to pay (18 to 20 percent interest every month) for the right to be slaves. We first become slaves to material things, then we become slaves to lenders who provide us the funds to buy those things through credit.

So God says, "Put me first, listen to what I say, pay attention to my words, don't go into debt, and I will make you prosper." (Notice also that He said there would be "no poor among you," if we followed this pattern.)

We as the people of God have strayed quite a ways from this commandment from God (not only as individuals, but also nationally; our national deficit is close to two trillion dollars, as is our consumer debt). We relinquish our personal freedom in Christ on the altar of debt; then we carry the same practice into God's ministries. Pastors, elders, trustees, deacons and other church leaders are caught up in this pattern of living, and it seems they reason that what is good for us personally and for our nation is good for God's local church and other types of ministries. We rationalize that the church must "step out in faith"; surely "God will provide." And this is true to a certain point. But we need to evaluate the issue of debt for churches. Such evaluation begins by looking at our individual viewpoints about personal debt.

What is your own personal position? Are you a lender or a borrower? That is, can you lend money because you have no debts? Paul the apostle, as well as other New Testament writers, called himself a slave of God. Whose slave are you?

When we put ourselves in debt, not only do we become slaves to the lender but we also violate another of God's warnings: we presume upon the future.

Before we can ever get a credit card or borrow from any lending institution we have to sign a contract that says we will make a given number of payments at a given monthly amount until all the obligation is paid. Most of the time, when churches borrow money from a lending institution, several members of the corporate board must co-sign that loan to assure that the debt will be paid. This is looking into the future for many years.

We face two situations that could lead to potential danger when we do this. The first is that we assume we are secure enough about the future to make such a commitment. The second is that we not only commit ourselves to a long-term debt, but we commit the future of those who are dependent upon us.

"Just a Vapor"

James spoke to the problem of presuming on the future when he told the church:

> Come now, you who say, "Today or tomorrow, we shall go to such and such a city, and spend a year there and engage in business and make a profit." Yet you do not know what your life will be like tomorrow. You are just a vapor that appears for a little while and then vanishes away (Jas. 4:13-14).

James, of course, is not talking about setting goals or making plans for the future, rather he means not to boast about our ability to continue to make a profit as we are now doing, or even to presume that we will increase our income. When we obligate ourselves, or our churches, for months or years in advance we are presuming that we will be able to meet our obligations. However, circumstances beyond our control—which we cannot know about when we sign these contracts— could cause us to default. Not being able to live up to our commitments is a poor witness

God says that He wants His people to depend on Him and not become slaves to the lender."

for us as Christians and completely devastating for our churches.

Inflation, Depression, Community Disasters

The second situation has to do with the pressures we exert on ourselves and our families when times become difficult because of debts we incurred years earlier. Sickness, job loss, and financial emergencies could prevent us from fulfilling our obligations, thus depriving those who depend on us of needs far greater than material "needs."

Think of the many stories you hear about an unexpected situation that rears its ugly head and throws an entire family into debt so deep they know they can never get out—medical expenses due to a serious, long-term illness; funeral expenses as a result of an unexpected death in the family; business or crop failure. When any of these disasters befall the primary wage earner, then all family members suffer financially for a long time. Not only financially, but they all have to bear the humiliation attendant upon staggering debt.

When the church encounters the unexpected—maybe something as simple as the loss of a powerful pastor, the same thing can happen. Inflation, depression, community disasters have all affected the pledges and financial commitments which church members have made toward a building program.

God says that He wants His people to depend on Him and not become slaves to the lender.

You may say, "That sounds very good. But what do we do when we have to make a major purchase? Few people can shovel over cash for a house."

We need to understand, at this point, the difference between borrowing and investing.

The Paradox of the "Investment Debt"

An investment debt is typically secured by the investment, and seldom do you incur personal liability. When a prudent man sets out to buy a house, in most cases he is already making rent payments each month. This debt is already part of his life. A house is not a luxury, it is a necessity and he knows that if he fails to meet the monthly obligation his family will not have a roof over their heads.

Since rent receipts have no financial value, if he rents for a long period of time all he will have to show for his faithfulness is a box of rent receipts. Here is where another factor enters in: stewardship.

Our tax laws are predicated on debt. Whether we agree or disagree with this concept is irrelevant. Those who owe the most get the biggest deductions. For example, the largest part of a house payment is made up of interest, which is tax deductible. Rent receipts are not tax deductible, and there is no potential growth of equity through increasing property values. Therefore, most Christian investment counselors consider mortgage debt an investment rather than a loan.

Even here, however, there is danger that we can get in over our heads. Too many people become slaves to their dwellings. Their home becomes their master—and in some cases, their god. They may spend too much for the house to begin with and soon find they have increasing monthly payments because of variable interest rates or higher property taxes.

Another thing people tend to do when they buy a home is immediately start "improving" it—landscaping, remodeling, new furnishings—until they have built up a debt rather than additional investment.

This is the way ministries also get into trouble. Most churches begin small. They rent until they can build up enough members and enough attendance to consider buying property. At this point, buying is good stewardship. It is better to invest God's money in something that will bring a return. Remember the Parable of the Talents?

So far, so good. The church finds a small piece of property they can afford, with maybe a little help from their denomination. They get simple plans for a sanctuary, or even start with an educational building that has a multipurpose room. They know that whatever they do to this point is still an investment because what they plan to build will easily cover the cost of the loan. The lending institutions are not concerned and neither are the faithful committed members.

Then one day they discover that their attendance has increased to the point where they know if they do not expand their facilities they will lose some of their people. They need more parking places; more Sunday School rooms; a bigger sanctuary. It is at this point where Satan steps in and begins his work. He reasons, "Things are going too good for these people, I'm losing ground." He begins to work on the senior pastor and convinces him that he must have something on the ball or people would not be pouring into his church. Maybe he can build an empire. Or perhaps the devil works in the hearts of the board.

The pastor and the board get together to talk about it. The plans start out reasonable enough. Someone says, "This neighborhood is really growing. They've started another new housing development over on Maple." Someone else says, "We really should be broadcasting on the radio. There are a lot of people who work Sunday mornings and can't get to church. And look how many senior citizens we have that can't drive." The pastor sits and listens with growing excitement. God is really moving in *his*, the pastor's, church.

You already know how the story turns out. The church ends up with so many "improvements" and such an ambitious building program that they have a hard time finding a lending institution that wants to take a chance on them. After all, the buildings could never be used for anything except a church, or maybe a school. What if the bank is forced, at some point in the future, to foreclose. But, finally, after trying several banks and savings and loan companies, the church gets their loan. They begin their buildings and at the same time they expand their ministry. "Let's strive to give 50 percent to missions next year." Or, "Pastor, you really ought to think about a TV ministry." And, "Our young people need a campground. The one for our denomination is just too far away." And so it goes.

Guidelines for Going into Investment Debt

As I said, in many cases, because of tax laws, going in debt by investing in property or other ways is good stewardship. Yet, even here there are proper ways of doing it. By following a few good ground rules you will not be a borrower but an investor.

First, *never invest money you cannot afford to part with.* All current ministry or family obligations should be considered before you incur any investment responsibility.

Second, I also believe that *you should not have any personal debt,* such as credit card balances, furniture payments, car payments, and the like—or like the church I spoke of before, a balloon payment coming up. Interest on personal debts can soon eat up any investment profit.

I also recommend that *you set aside liquid assets—*

Keys to ministry success for you personally, for your business, and for your church or other ministry . . . come directly from the Owner's Manual, the Bible."

money in the bank—for standard living or operating
expenses for at least six months. The amount will vary
depending on your own personal or ministry's needs.

Next, *seek wise counsel.* It is critical that you understand the need to discuss any investment program with
professional advisors. Do not rely on tips or advice from a
good friend, fellow pastor or inexperienced counselor—
especially not if he or she has a get-rich-quick scheme. If it
sounds too good to be true, it probably is.

*Understand the difference between investments and per-
sonal money management.* Personal money management
means that you handle your financial affairs in such a way
that you do not go into debt. Learning to live within your
income is the key to good money management.

Personal money management also includes *preparing
for the time when you will not have to work for your money,*
but your money will work for you. This applies more to
you personally than to your ministry. Once your personal
money management is under control and discretionary dollars are available, then and only then can investment
become a viable option.

There is more that applies to a church investing in the
future. The next chapter will cover keys to ministry success for you personally, for your business, and for your
church or other ministry. All these keys come directly
from the Owner's Manual, the Bible.

11

When All Else Fails, Read the Instructions

Some time ago, I had the opportunity to work with a businessman who had been asked to help a large ministry solve some of its staggering financial problems. On the surface the task looked insurmountable; their debts were huge and most of them were long overdue. Creditors were threatening some pretty dire consequences if they were not paid at once. The pressure on the pastor and his staff was so severe that they were hindered from ministering effectively.

Those of us who were called in to help the church had a very distinct advantage: Anything we did could only help, the church was at the bottom of the well and could go no deeper.

Every approach to solving the problems had been attempted by others before us to no avail; indeed the problems only became worse. We were just about the last hope the ministry had.

We began by doing the obvious. We had prayer meetings, held banquets, wrote letters—did everything that had helped other ministries get out of trouble.

Nothing did the job.

When we finally got to the end of our rope, we decided it was time to read the instructions: We went to God's how-to book, the Bible. Why is it we seem to go to the Source of power only after everything else has been tried?

Personal Testimony

Fifteen years ago I would never have considered the Bible as a financial guide. During the past decade, however, my attitudes and ideas on management and success have undergone major surgery. Since I met Jesus Christ and accepted Him as my personal Savior I have come to many new conclusions. One of the most important is that I can do nothing worthwhile without God; but with Him I can accomplish things I never would have attempted years ago. But I also have learned that to find the solutions it is important that I not only know *Him* but that I also know *His Word.*

My library still contains a number of how-to books, most of them written by men of the world. Some of them have words of real wisdom and should not be ignored. But in the past few years I find more and more that I bypass the popular books on how to succeed in business or how to manage effectively. I now find that I almost always turn to the one book on management that has yet to be wrong: the Bible.

My businessman friend and I finally did just that when we found we were no closer to solving the financial problems of this large ministry. We came up with a plan that encompassed 30 Scripture references in the Bible.

Of course, it does you no good just to read these passages, you also have to do what they tell you to do and live the way they tell you to live. This is not easy; it requires the power and encouragement of the Holy Spirit. But if you decide to run your personal life, your business, or your church by these 30 steps, I assure you that your life and the life of your organization will change. I challenge you to try. You have everything to gain and nothing to lose.

Thirty Steps to Success

Step number 1: *Become familiar with Scripture.*

In Matthew 4:1-10 we find Jesus, after His baptism and anointing with the Holy Spirit, being led into the wilderness to undergo "forty days and forty nights" of temptation by Satan. Satan was determined to get Jesus to sin so that God's plan for the redemption of man would fail.

The Bible records only three examples of these temptations, but we know that Jesus was "tempted in all things as we are, yet without sin" (Heb. 4:15). In each case, here in the wilderness, Jesus responded to the temptation with the Word of God.

> The tempter came and said to Him, "If you are the Son of God, command that these stones become bread." But He answered and said, "It is written, 'Man shall not live on bread alone, but on every word that proceeds out of the mouth of God.'"
> Then the devil took Him into the holy city; and he stood Him on the pinnacle of the temple, and said to Him, "If You are the Son of God throw Yourself down; for it is written, 'He will give His angels charge concerning you; and on

You cannot expect God's Word to help you if you do not know what it has to say to you."

their hands they will bear you up, lest you strike your foot against a stone.'" Jesus said to him, "On the other hand, it is written, 'You shall not tempt the Lord your God.'"

Again, the devil took Him to a very high mountain, and showed Him all the kingdoms of the world, and their glory; and he said to Him, "All these things will I give You, if You fall down and worship me." Then Jesus said to him, "Begone, Satan! For it is written, 'You shall worship the Lord your God, and serve Him only'" (Matt. 4:3-10).

Notice one thing about this incident: Satan also used Scripture, or rather, he misused Scripture. Step number 1 also includes knowing Bible verses in their proper context and using them correctly. Some people will quote Benjamin Franklin or Shakespeare and call it Scripture. You cannot expect God's Word to help you if you do not know what it has to say to you. *Become familiar with Scripture.*

Step number 2: *Be willing to be blessed, do not have false humility.*

After Jesus gave the Parable of the Unmerciful Slave He left Galilee and went to Judea (Matt. 19:1-2). As He traveled to Judea, "great multitudes followed Him, and He healed them there" (v. 2). The crowds of people were willing to travel long distances to be with Jesus, to hear His teachings, *to be blessed,* and to be healed.

Often we deprive ourselves of blessing from God because (1) we are not willing to go long distances or (2) we refuse to be open to His blessings. Look for God's blessings. He wants to bless you; He is waiting to bless you.

Step number 3: *Do not borrow.*

As we saw in Deuteronomy 15:6, God has directed us not to borrow so that we will not be slaves to the lender. Proverbs 22:7 says:

> The rich rules over the poor, and the borrower becomes the lender's slave.

Solomon spells out God's warning very clearly. To use credit in business and the leverage of investments under the right conditions may be good stewardship; however, borrowing for wants—for things that depreciate or are consumable—is not good stewardship. Invest wisely, but *do not borrow.*

Step number 4: *Do not be a security for others.*

You have been prudent, your credit is good. If you needed to you could borrow from many sources. Those of us with good credit ratings often receive offers in the mail from lending institutions telling us that a certain amount of money is available to us to help us buy now those things we want without having to wait for some time in the future. Those who do not need the money or are cautious about how they use their money are usually the ones who are approached about borrowing.

A friend whose rating is not as high and who cannot borrow money as easily as you may approach you asking you to co-sign a note for him. He is a good Christian friend, and you want to help him. What does God's Word say about this?

> Do not be a man who strikes hands in pledge or puts up security for debts; if you lack the means to pay, your very bed will be snatched from under you (Prov. 22:26-27, *NIV*).

Do not co-sign for another person; however, that is not the end of the matter. God has something else to say to you concerning a brother who may be having financial difficulties. John, in his first Epistle, says:

> Whoever has this world's goods, and beholds his brother in need and closes his heart against him, how does the love of God abide in him? (1 John 3:17)

While you are not supposed to co-sign for a loan, you are supposed to share what you have with a brother who is in need. You are supposed to *give* your help.

Many good friendships have broken up because Christians did not heed the admonition from Solomon in Proverbs. *Do not be a security for others.*

Step number 5: *Be generous to the poor.*

The Bible tells us that the borrower is the lender's slave, but in Proverbs 19:17 we are told that when we are generous to the poor we are a lender to God.

> He who is gracious to the poor man lends to the LORD, and He will repay him for his good deed.

Not only are we to be slaves to the Lord, but we also have the privilege of being a lender to the Lord. Think about it! *Be generous to the poor.*

Step number 6: *Pay your bills and pay them on time.*

One sure indication that you are having financial problems, whether personally or in a ministry, is whether or not you are behind in paying your bills. Cash flow slows, bills do not get paid on time and soon creditors are either adding late charges to the bill or beginning to complain, or both. You or your ministry will soon find you have become a poor credit risk and your witness has been destroyed.

Heed the word of the Lord concerning paying your bills:

> Look! The wages you failed to pay the workmen who mowed your fields are crying out against you. The cries of the harvesters have reached the ears of the Lord Almighty (Jas. 5:4, *NIV*).

It does not get any easier if you hold onto your bills until later. Obviously, if you cannot pay your bills you are spending too much money on other things. *Pay your bills and pay them on time.*

Step number 7: *Transfer ownership back to the Lord.*

God created the earth, He made you, and He owns the world "and all that is in it" (Ps. 50:12, *NIV*). Proverbs 16:3 tells you how you can prosper in what you do:

> Commit your works to the LORD, and your plans
> will be established.

If we are to succeed and prosper we must be careful not to become possessive of what God has given us to manage. *Transfer ownership back to the Lord.*

Step number 8: *Be diligent.*

When a person is described as being diligent we often think of one who is hard working and perseveres in whatever he or she does. This is also what Solomon meant in Proverbs 10:4:

Poor is he who works with a negligent hand, but
the hand of the diligent makes rich.

How often do we start out a job with much enthusiasm, but as time goes by our enthusiasm wanes—and so
does our diligence. We tend to get negligent, but God says
to *be diligent* and He will prosper us.

Step 9: *Learn to Pray.*

"Religious" people seem to believe that God is terribly
concerned about what they can do for God—in the Old
Testament the people gave sacrifices; in the New Testament the Pharisaical rules and regulations were what people thought God wanted; today it is how "good" we can be
for God, or how much we "do" for Him. What does God
say about all this?

The sacrifice of the wicked is an abomination to
the LORD, but the prayer of the upright is His
delight . . . . The Lord is far from the wicked,
but He hears the prayer of the righteous (Prov.
15:8,29).

God is not as interested in our "great" sacrifices and
works as He is in prayers from our righteous and upright
hearts. We must *learn to pray.*

Step number 10: *Learn to manage yourself.*

Paul spoke several times about having self-control. In
1 Corinthians he used the example of an athlete who had to
use self-control in all things in order to compete in the
games; in Galatians 5:23 he names self-control as a fruit of
the Spirit; then in 2 Timothy 1:7 he says that God Himself
has given us "power and love and discipline," or self-
control or sound judgment.

Solomon also spoke about self-control:

> Like a city that is broken into and without walls
> is a man who has no control over his spirit
> (Prov. 25:28).

It is a fact of life that even when we know what is right we tend to do what we know we should not. We must *learn to manage ourselves,* to have self-control.

Step number 11: *Be just and do not cheat.*
Throughout Scripture we are told that the little things are what counts. When we fail in the little responsibilities we will eventually find ourselves failing in the big picture. This is particularly true as it relates to how we rationalize our debts and our obligations toward others. God has called us to be His representatives and it is an abomination to Him when we cheat even in little things. Solomon said:

> The Lord abhors dishonest scales, but accurate
> weights are his delight (Prov. 11:1, *NIV*).

Even in the little things we are supposed to *be just and not cheat.*

Step number 12: *Plan ahead.*
The old cliché of "plan your work and work your plan" is not just from man, Scripture also tells us to do this.

> The plans of the diligent lead surely to advan-
> tage, but everyone who is hasty comes surely
> to poverty (Prov. 21:5).

Our plans are important (this goes along with step

number 8, be diligent). God does not intend us to do His work haphazardly. Some people do not plan because they feel they will interfere with the guidance of the Holy Spirit; but Jesus said the Holy Spirit is one who is called alongside to help us. We make the best plans we can, keeping in mind what God is calling us to do, and the Holy Spirit will enable us by His power to fulfill them. Do not be afraid or neglect to *plan ahead.*

Step number 13: *Do not waste time on retribution.*

Many people use so much energy living in the past, harboring grudges, that they have no time or inclination to live in the present or plan for the future. Nothing will hinder positive output like wanting to "get even."

Do not say, "I will repay evil"; wait for the Lord, and He will save you (Prov. 20:22).

Harboring a grudge is a waste of time and accomplishes nothing but bad feelings. *Do not waste time on retribution.*

Step number 14: *Get all the facts before you act.*

"Don't confuse me with facts" is often said tongue-in-cheek. However, we have all been in a position where our minds are made up and we do not want to have to change them. Solomon says about this:

He who gives an answer before he hears, it is folly and shame to him (Prov. 18:13).

The word from the Lord is *get all the facts before you act.*

Step number 15: *Seek wise counsel.*

We have already talked in this book about the importance of seeking wise counsel. We need each other. Each person has a gift to share that is different from the next person's gift. When we get together and share our gifts, and listen to the experience and wisdom of others, then we can get a clearer picture of what we are supposed to do.

> Where there is no guidance, the people fall, but in abundance of counselors there is victory (Prov. 11:14).

As slaves to the Lord we must learn to *seek wise counsel,* and then heed it.

Step number 16: *Expect to be compensated for your work.*

We all admire men and women of God who serve in a ministry without expecting compensation. We tend to say, "How noble he is"; "Isn't she humble!" However, when a person works for nothing, all too often that is what the work is considered to be worth—nothing.

The Apostle Paul spoke about getting paid for your work:

> Who at any time serves as a soldier at his own expense? Who plants a vineyard, and does not eat the fruit of it? Or who tends a flock and does not use the milk of the flock? I am not speaking these things according to human judgment, am I? Or does not the Law also say these things? For it is written in the Law of Moses, "You shall not muzzle the ox while he is threshing." God is not concerned about oxen, is He? Or is He speaking altogether for our sake? Yes, for our

sake it was written, because the plowman
ought to plow in hope, and the thresher to
thresh in hope of sharing the crops (1 Cor. 9:7-
10).

And something else to consider is the precedent you
set by working for nothing. The next person called on to
do that job may not be able to afford to work for nothing.
Expect to be compensated for your work.

Step number 17: *Select your business associates with
care.*

As Christians we tend to see other Christians through
rose-colored glasses. We must accept the fact that Christians come in all shapes and sizes, as well as in all levels of
ability. When choosing a business associate you should
consider more than whether or not he or she is a Christian; your business partner should be one you can respect
and work with harmoniously.

Like a bad tooth and an unsteady foot is confi-
dence in a faithless man in time of trouble
(Prov. 25:19).

Select your business associates with care.

Step number 18: *Tell the truth.*
"Speak truth, each one of you, with his neighbor, for
we are members of one another" (Eph. 4:25). How easy it
is to stretch the truth. A little white lie cannot do any
harm, can it? As Pat Robertson said, "Evangelistically
speaking" has come to mean stretching the truth.

A worthless person, a wicked man, is the one
who walks with a false mouth, who winks with

his eyes, who signals with his feet, who points with his fingers; who with perversity in his heart devises evil continually, who spreads strife. Therefore his calamity will come suddenly; instantly he will be broken, and there will be no healing (Prov. 6:12-15).

If we are to succeed personally and in our ministry we will *tell the truth.*

Step number 19: *Actively despise evil.*

In Proverbs 8:13, Solomon warns against "evil" such as pride, arrogance and a perverted mouth. How many of the Glitter Gospel evangelists have gotten in trouble because of these three "evils"? In Romans 12:9, Paul said to "abhor what is evil"; and in 1 Thessalonians 5:22 he says to "abstain from every form of evil."

To fear the Lord is to hate evil; I hate pride and arrogance, evil behavior and perverse speech (Prov. 8:13, *NIV*).

A Christian who wishes to prosper must *actively despise evil,* especially pride, arrogance and perverse speech.

Step number 20: *Protect your reputation.*

I once heard a testimony from a man in Christ's ministry who said he was parked at a red light, waiting for it to change, when the person behind him started honking at him. He took it for a few seconds, then got out of his car and walked back to demand angrily, "What's your problem?" The young lady said, "Your bumper sticker says, 'Honk if you love Jesus,' so I did."

To give way to what you know is wrong
will soon lead to a polluted soul."

When we advertise that we belong to Christ, we must be especially careful to guard our reputations because whatever we do reflects on the Lord's name. Proverbs 22:1 says:

A good name is more desired than great riches,
favor is better than silver and gold.

Protect your reputation and you protect Christ's name.

Step number 21: *Be subject to authority.*
The higher a person goes in an organization the less inclined he is to answer to authority; he, as leader, becomes the authority. But remember, there is always someone else a little higher on the ladder than you are.

Let every person be in subjection to the governing authorities. For there is no authority except from God, and those which exist are established by God. Therefore, he who resists authority has opposed the ordinance of God; and they who have opposed will receive condemnation upon themselves (Rom. 13:1,2).

A person who recognizes that governing authorities are established by God will obey the laws of the land concerning doing business and paying taxes and will not try to circumvent his obligation. *Be subject to authority.*

Step number 22: *Do not compromise your standards.*
Many business people get into trouble when they feel it is necessary to compromise their standards for one reason or another. Solomon said this about compromising:

Like a muddied spring or a polluted well is a
righteous man who gives way to the wicked
(Prov. 25:26, *NIV*).

To give way to what you know is wrong will soon lead
to a polluted soul. Often we begin to compromise when we
start to "believe our own publicity" or when we think too
highly of ourselves to the point where we are above conforming to high standards. I believe this is what Solomon
meant in verse 27 of this same chapter: "It is not good to
eat too much honey, nor is it honorable to seek one's own
honor" (v. 27, *NIV*).

Keep your standards high; as Paul said: "Let us keep
living by that same standard to which we have attained"
(Phil. 3:16).

Step number 23: *Do not limit what God has promised.*

The Bible is full of promises that God has given us.
Most of His promises come with a condition; but if we fulfill the condition, God's promises are released to us. However, it is always possible to limit God by doubt and fear.
When you limit God you limit yourself.

Jesus, in John 10, gave His disciples the Parable of the
Sheepfold then followed it up with the Parable of the Good
Shepherd. Between these two parables He said:

I came that they [you] might have life, and
might have it abundantly (v. 10).

God wants us to have abundant life, and this means to
be successful in our personal and business ventures. *Do
not limit God's promises.*

Step number 24: *Confirm that your plans check out
with God's Word.*

When Paul was warning Timothy about the "difficult times" that were ahead for the ministry, he gave Timothy a list of instructions to follow and things to beware of. One of the things he said was to

> continue in the things you have learned . . . [because they are] sacred writings which are able to give you . . . wisdom. . . . All Scripture is inspired by God and profitable for teaching, for reproof, for correction, for training in righteousness (2 Tim. 3:14-16).

As we plan ahead and set our goals we must be sure that all our actions are in God's will. Scripture gives us His plan and His goals. We need to *confirm that our plans check out with God's Word.*

Step number 25: *Meditate upon the Word.*
Not only should we check out all our plans to see that they conform with God's plans for our lives, but we need to continue to seek His will in the daily administration of all our affairs.

> How blessed is the man who does not walk in the counsel of the wicked, nor stand in the path of sinners, nor sit in the seat of scoffers! But his delight is in the law of the Lord, and in His law he meditates day and night. And he will be like a tree firmly planted by streams of water, which yields its fruit in its season, and its leaf does not wither; and in whatever he does, he prospers (Ps. 1:1-3).

How can you avoid burnout, rust out, and wear out? *Meditate on the Word of God.*

Step number 26: *Be willing to change your plan.*

Suppose in your checking and meditating you discover that the plan you have established and nourished is not the one God would have you follow? No problem; be willing to switch gears and go another direction. One of the best examples we have in the New Testament of a switch of plans is that of Joseph moving to a different country when the angel came to him and told him Jesus was in danger.

> And [Joseph] arose and took the Child and His mother by night, and departed for Egypt; and was there until the death of Herod . . . . But when Herod was dead, behold, an angel of the Lord appeared in a dream to Joseph in Egypt, saying, "Arise and take the Child and His mother, and go into the land of Israel; for those who sought the Child's life are dead." And he arose and took the Child and His mother, and came into the land of Israel. But when he heard that Archelaus was reigning over Judea in place of his father Herod, he was afraid to go there; and being warned by God in a dream, he departed for the regions of Galilee (Matt. 2:14,15,19-22).

Hear the Lord and be willing to do as He says, even if it runs contrary to your present plans. Joseph changed plans three times. *Be willing to change your plan.*

Step number 27: *Be patient yet persistent.*

How often do you wonder what you are doing wrong, why you are not getting anywhere, when this person over here is not as honest or hardworking as you are, yet he is succeeding and you are barely off the ground? David has a word for you:

> Be still before the Lord and wait patiently for him; do not fret when men succeed in their ways, when they carry out their wicked schemes (Ps. 37:7, *NIV*).

Do not give into the ways of the world or let others' prosperity cause you to flag in your efforts. Keep moving forward, trust God's Word and God's timing. *Be patient yet persistent.*

Step number 28: *Give God His tithe.*
All you have in your business or ministry belongs to God. Show your appreciation by following His command to give Him a tenth right off the top of your profit.

> You shall surely tithe all the produce from what you sow, which comes out of the field every year (Deut. 14:22).

Your obedience, honesty, diligence, and patience are critical; so is your tithe. *Give God His tithe.*

Step number 29: *Seek God's Kingdom first.*
As we get close to the end of the list we need to remember that it is easy to get our priorities mixed up. Matthew 6:33 tells us what comes first:

> Seek first His kingdom, and His righteousness; and all these things shall be added to you.

When we start out this way, the rest will follow. *Seek God's Kingdom first.*

Step number 30: *Remember that God is with you even when things are tough.*

When we start our Christian walk, we more or less expect a rose garden. Then we begin to discover the thorns. Every day is not the high we thought it was going to be. We have increasing pressures and we still make mistakes. We feel like the Apostle Paul when he said, in essence, "Why is it that I do what I don't want to do, and I fail to do what I do want to do?" (see Rom. 7:19).

I cannot speak for you, but I can assure you that I often ask that question of myself. It is then that I remember that:

> Unless a grain of wheat falls into the earth and dies, it remains by itself alone; but if it dies, it bears much fruit (John 12:24).

Even if the going gets tough it does not mean that God is not still at work in our lives. If we read the instructions in the Owner's Manual we will succeed and prosper.

Postscript
The Handwriting on the Wall

"That which has been is that which will be, and that which has been done is that which will be done. So, there is nothing new under the sun" (Eccles. 1:9). These words of the Preacher in the book of Ecclesiastes never rang truer than they have for the Church in this decade.

Even though we have the lessons from history we still repeat "that which has been done." Solomon, the Preacher who spoke these words, was "wiser than all men," yet he became trapped in the very same things that entrap our "preachers" of today—wealth, fame, and self-indulgence. God was willing to give Solomon anything he asked for, the only condition being that he would always remain true to Him. And Jesus said that those of us in His Body would also have all things in abundance, but like Solomon we need to put Him first if we want these blessings to continue.

The entire Christian world is suffering from recent bad publicity brought on by the actions of a major TV ministry.

(Madalyn Murray O'Hair said she believed it was all a plot to get more publicity.) In this last chapter I feel that I need to speak more in depth on the rise and fall of Jim and Tammy Bakker and the ministry they managed for God. I do this with extreme concern; not to sling mud or cause more hurt for the many who have been affected by this disaster, but to help all of us examine what brought about their fall and, hopefully, to learn from it.

Soaring on the Wings of Religious Fervor

In the December 17, 1973, issue of *U.S. News and World Report* is an article entitled "Test for Big Churches." The subtitle states, "Developing in a troubled America is a new wave of religious fervor—the seeking of answers in emotional experience, not formalized worship."[1]

The magazine went on for over two pages telling readers that a new wave of evangelism is gaining converts across America. It stated that "what is developing in some ways is a replay of an earlier era when tent meeting evangelism brought unbelievers down the sawdust trail." Churches used as examples of this new surge included The Church on the Way in Van Nuys, California, that had dwindled to about 25 people five years before but now had grown to 1,200 per service in five services every Sunday; Melodyland Christian Center in Anaheim, California, exemplified as the very center of the new wave with 1,000 converts per year and three Sunday services in an auditorium that seats more than 4,000; Calvary Chapel in Costa Mesa, California, that had just moved into its new 11-acre facility with a meeting hall that could accommodate more than 2,000 people, and they already required three Sunday services and closed circuit television in an adjoining hall.

What an exciting time! God was doing a great work and man could take little credit for it. The article closed with:

> Given the present conditions in the U.S. and the rest of the world, . . . the resurgence of interest in old and new religions seem likely to continue with undiminished force for some time to come.[2]

That "some time to come" lasted barely 15 years. The subject of the May 25, 1987 U.S. News and World Report was not about religious enthusiasm and hope for a world in trouble, rather it was about an outstanding ministry that got its priorities confused; they practiced the philosophy of "bigger must be better" rather than recognizing that bigger indicated the blessings of God. This attitude is reflected in the report:

> "We must raise $7 million between today and May 31 or this ministry will be in dire jeopardy." The Reverend Jerry Falwell, warning viewers of "The PTL Club" that they must donate $20 million to $25 million over the next 90 days to save the TV ministry founded by Jim Bakker.[3]

In the same issue of this popular magazine, on the "Washington Whispers" page was a report that the Bakker scandal was eroding the presidential campaign of Pat Robertson. Pollsters said Robertson's popularity ratings were diving, even though he was not involved in the Bakker affair.[4]

In a few short years a major news magazine has given us the history of how "religious fervor" was quenched

Christians have become so separated from the world that we think everyone who is not one of us is against us. God has used the world to warn Christians before. This time, we just were not listening."

because of a ministry that got its priorities confused, moved out of God's will, and began to exploit their "partners." Not only did they help to quench the work of God worldwide, they also profaned the name of the Lord and damaged the chances of a brother in Christ who was considering running as a presidential contender.

All this could have been avoided if God's people had heeded God's warnings from Scripture, from modern-day prophets, and from the secular press—of all places. Many newspaper articles, some dating back to the mid-seventies, indicated that PTL was having problems. Of course, these reports were denied by the Bakkers, and the Christian community elected to believe the Bakkers and not the press. Why? Because we *trusted* that our fellow believers who were so "successful" in the "work of the Lord" would not lie to us. We were sure the press was out to get them because the Bakkers said so.

Jesus, in His prayer in the garden, prayed that God would not take His followers "out of the world, but to keep them from the evil one" because "they are not of this world, even as I am not of this world" (John 17:15,16). But Christians have become so separated from the world that we think everyone who is not one of us is against us. God has used the world to warn Christians before. This time, we just were not listening.

Warning from Concerned Journalists

Jeff Prugh and Russell Chandler, religion editors for the *Los Angeles Times* newspaper wrote an article that was published in the May 20, 1979, edition of the *Times* that was headed "Old-Time Religion in the Big Time."

After describing the near circus-like atmosphere of a typical telecast of PTL—that boasted four $100,000 color cameras, a 30-monitor control booth, and 60 men and women in four tiers answering constantly ringing telephones from people who needed prayer or wanted to contribute to the telecast—the article gave some background of the ministry. They told about the annual budget of $45 million. They mentioned that in March of that year Bakker had tearfully told his viewers that his network was millions of dollars in debt. He said unless donations increased he would soon be off the air.

Then the article reported that in April the FCC began to investigate the possible misuse of funds by the officers of the PTL Club.[5]

Remember, this article was written in 1979; yet, the Christian community paid no attention to what could be described as "prophetic" warning signs.

The Apostle Paul told the church at Thessalonica not to "despise prophetic utterances. But examine everything carefully; hold fast to that which is good; abstain from every form of evil" (1 Thess. 5:20-22). We do not have to believe everything the media tells us, but we should be alert to possible problems involving God's work.

The *Los Angeles Times* article had more to say about Bakker. After telling PTL backers that they were "giving every penny of our life savings to keep PTL from collapsing," Bakker reportedly made a $6,000 down payment on a houseboat.[6]

This article by the *Los Angeles Times* religion editor was not the first newspaper to take the Bakkers to task. The North Carolina *Charlotte Observer* had challenged the Bakkers for a number of years. Of course, few of us even knew about it; most of those who did, paid little attention to what the newspaper reported. Soon, however, the wire services picked up accounts of PTL excesses and larger newspapers began to look into possible follow-up stories;

it became harder *not* to find an article in most major newspapers about the Bakkers and their life-styles and woes. Still, Christians did nothing to avert the tragedy that followed a few years later.

Also in 1979, the *Wall Street Journal* ran a feature article headlined, "Faith Fails to Keep Money Woes Away from a TV Ministry—Rev. Bakker's Free Spending Is Blamed for Difficulties."

The *Wall Street Journal* article goes into some length on the problems of an FCC investigation into PTL's handling of its finances and discusses mounting debts of the organization.

The red warning flag had progressed from the hometown newspaper in North Carolina to a major newspaper in Los Angeles to a national newspaper that is read throughout the English speaking world. Yet we still did not heed the warning.

Warning from Christian Periodicals

By 1984 even the Christian media was talking about the peccadillos of the Bakkers.

Christianity Today reported that the Bakkers stayed in a hotel in Florida at a cost of $1,000 per night. Yet how many readers were concerned enough that the tithes and offerings of a lot of little people, some maybe near the poverty level, were paying for a potentate life-style? Why were Jim and Tammy Bakker not called to account for these repeated excesses? One has to wonder at the gullibility or naiveté of the Christian community that continued to respond to the pleadings for more and more money.

Well, you say, after all, what could *I* have done except not send the ministry any of my tithes or offerings? There are a few other things you could have done. You could have written letters to PTL exhorting them to be better stewards of God's money. There is something else you can still do—not to help a situation that may be beyond saving, but to help prevent such a thing happening to a ministry you support. Jamie Buckingham put it well:

> I can't do much about the garbage which comes through the TV tube in the name of Jesus, nor have I been very effective in stemming the tide of mail which comes from Bible-waving, Mercedes-driving beggars. But I can make certain that the leadership in our local body does not manipulate.[8]

"Immorality . . . Which Amounts to Idolatry"

There were some very serious accusations made against Jim Bakker involving his personal morality, some of which he admitted. Jim must answer to his Father in heaven concerning these things. Paul told the Colossians that they were to "consider the members of your earthly body as dead to immorality, impurity, passion, evil desire, and greed, which amounts to idolatry" (Col. 3:5). The primary thing that brought Solomon down was idolatry. Jim Bakker may be guilty of idolatry not only in the way Paul describes it but also in his extravagant life-style.

Jim and Tammy Bakker owe the Body of Christ an apology for their violation of the Body's trust and for the violation of God's Word.

Even as I write this the newspapers are carrying conflicting information: Jim and Tammy Bakker claim they are going to return to PTL; PTL's new management is preparing to file bankruptcy because the ministry is $72 million in debt. The Body of Christ is still suffering dismemberment.

Daniel 5:22-30 tells about another leader who had everything the world could offer—wealth, power, and an example of a good ruler who preceded him. God said to him:

> Yet you . . . have not humbled your heart . . .
> but you have exalted yourself against the Lord
> of heaven (vv. 22-23).

It was then that Belshazzar, the king, saw the handwriting on the wall: *"Mene, mene, tekel upharsin,"* which meant that God had numbered his kingdom and put an end to it; Belshazzar had been weighed on the scales and was found wanting. If God were to weigh your ministry today, would He find it wanting?

The damage to the Body has been painful; however, if we all begin now to heed God's warnings from whatever source they come, we will eventually weather this current storm and begin to see a silver lining around the dark clouds.

Read the steps in chapter 11 again. Commit yourself to following these steps for your personal life first, and then extend them to your own local church. The Church looks bad right now, but if we remember our "first love," as Revelation 2:4-5 says, and "remember the height from which [we] have fallen" and "repent and do the things [we] did at first," then "to him who overcomes, [God] will give the right to eat from the tree of life, which is in the paradise of God" (v. 7, *NIV*).

Appendices
The Donor's Bill of Rights

Make sure your charity's standards and guidelines assure you of a "bill of rights" as a donor. You have the right to:

1. Know how the funds of an organization are being spent.
2. Know what the programs you support are accomplishing.
3. Know that the organization is in compliance with federal, state and municipal laws.
4. Restrict or designate your gifts to a particular project.
5. A response to your inquiries about finances and programs.
6. Visit offices and program sites of an organization to talk personally with the staff.
7. Not be high pressured into giving to any organization.
8. Know that the organization is well managed.
9. Know that there is a responsible governing board and who those board members are.

10. Know that all appeals for funds are truthful and accurate.

Remember, the *important point* is that *all* charities should practice sound financial accounting. Good charities willingly answer tough questions before you give. Nonprofit organizations, therefore, should be willing to supply this information to you prior to any gift:

- Does the organization have a clear and strong commitment to a certain project area?
- Has it established an independent board to meet specific requirements, and does the board accept responsibility for the activities of the organization?
- Are its books audited annually by certified public accountants?
- Does the charity practice full disclosure? Will it provide a copy of its audited financial statements to anyone who requests one? Upon request, will it provide information to donors about any program that the donors have supported?
- How does the organization avoid conflicts of interest?
- Does the charity adhere to strict guidelines and standards for fund raising? (Note the recommended "Standards for Fund Raising" and "Standards of Responsible Stewardship" of the Evangelical Council for Financial Accountability on the following pages.)
- Do they have an annual review procedure to be certain they stay in compliance with those guidelines and standards?

Adapted from "The Giver's Guide," published by the Evangelical Council for Financial Accountability, P.O. Box 17511, Washington, DC 20041. Used by permission.

Standards of Responsible Stewardship of the Evangelical Council for Financial Accountability

1. Every member organization shall subscribe to a written statement of faith clearly affirming its commitment to the evangelical Christian faith and shall conduct its financial operations in a manner which reflects generally accepted Christian practices.
2. Every member organization shall be governed by a responsible board, a majority of whom shall not be employees/staff, and/or related by blood or marriage, which shall meet at least semiannually to establish policy and review its accomplishments.
3. Every member organization shall obtain an annual audit performed by an independent public accounting firm in accordance with generally accepted auditing standards (GAAS) with financial statements prepared in accordance with generally accepted accounting principles (GAAP).
4. Every member organization shall have a functioning audit review committee appointed by the board, a

majority of whom shall not be employees/staff, and/or related by blood or marriage, for the purpose of reviewing the annual audit and reporting its findings to the board.

5. Every member organization shall provide a copy of its current audited financial statements upon written request.

6. Every member organization shall conduct its activities with the highest standards of financial integrity.

7. Every member organization shall comply with each of the ECFA Standards for Fund Raising.

—Used by permission of the Evangelical Council for Financial Accountability, P.O. Box 17511, Washington, DC 20041.

Standards for Fund Raising of the Evangelical Council for Financial Accountability

1. *Truthfulness in Communication.* All representations of fact, description of financial condition of the organization, or narrative about events must be current, complete and accurate. References to past activities or events must be appropriately dated. There must be no material omissions or exaggerations of fact or use of misleading photographs or any other communication which would tend to create a false impression or misunderstanding.

2. *Communication and Donor Expectations.* Fund raising must not create unrealistic donor expectations of what a donor's gift will actually accomplish within the limits of the organization's ministry.

3. *Communication and Donor Intent.* All statements made by the organization in its fund raising appeals about the use of the gift must be honored by the organization. The donor's intent is related to both what was

communicated in the appeal and to any donor instructions accompanying the gift. The organization should be aware that communications made in fund raising appeals may create a legally binding restriction.

4. *Projects Unrelated to a Ministry's Primary Purpose.* An organization raising or receiving funds for programs that are not part of its present or prospective ministry, but are proper in accordance with its exempt purpose, must either treat them as restricted funds and channel them through an organization that can carry out the donor's intent, or return the funds to the donor.

5. *Incentives and Premiums.* Fund raising appeals which, in exchange for a contribution, offer premiums or incentives (the value of which is not insubstantial, but which is significant in relation to the amount of the donation) must advise the donor, both in the solicitation and in the receipt, of the fair market value of the premium or incentive and that the value is not deductible for tax purposes.

6. *Reporting.* An organization must provide, on request, a report, including financial information, on the project for which it is soliciting gifts.

7. *Percentage Compensation for Fund Raisers.* Compensation of outside fund raising consultants based directly or indirectly on a percentage of what is raised, or on any other contingency agreement, may create potential conflicts and opportunities for abuse. Full disclosure of such arrangements is required, at least annually, in the organization's audited financial statements, in which the disclosure must match income and related expenses. Compensation to the organization's own employees on a percentage basis or contingency basis is not allowed.

8. *Tax Deductible Gifts for a Named Recipient's Personal Benefit.* Tax deductible gifts may not be used to pass

money or benefits to any named individual for personal use.

9. *Conflict of Interest on Royalties.* An officer, director, or other principal of the organization must not receive royalties for any product that is used for fund raising or promotional purposes by his/her own organization.

10. *Acknowledgement of Gifts in Kind.* Property or gifts in kind received by an organization, should be acknowledged describing the property or gift accurately without a statement of the gift's market value. It is the responsibility of the donor to determine the fair market value of the property for tax purposes. But the organization should inform the donor of IRS reporting requirements for all gifts in excess of $5,000.

11. *Acting in the Interest of the Donor.* An organization must make every effort to avoid accepting a gift from or entering into a contract with a prospective donor which would knowingly place a hardship on the donor, or place the donor's future well-being in jeopardy.

12. *Financial Advice.* The representative of the organization, when dealing with persons regarding commitments on major estate assets, must seek to guide and advise donors so they have adequately considered the broad interests of the family and the various ministries they are currently supporting before they make a final decision. Donors should be encouraged to use the services of their attorneys, accountants, or other professional advisors.

—Used by permission of the Evangelical Council for Financial Accountability, P.O. Box 17511, Washington, DC 20041.

Notes

Preface

1. *Redding Record Searchlight,* March 24, 1987, Update: Nation.
2. *U.S. News & World Report,* March 23, 1987, p. 10.
3. Russell Chandler, "Bakker Scandal Damages Standing of TV Preachers," *Los Angeles Times,* March 31, 1987, Part 1, p. 1.
4. Jamie Buckingham, "God Is Shaking the Church," *Charisma,* June, 1987, p. 20.

Chapter 1

1. John Dart, "Park That PTL Built Rides Roller-Coaster of Success, Scandal," *Los Angeles Times,* March 30, 1987, p. 3.

Chapter 2

1. *Presbyterian Layman,* Aug.-Sept., p. 1.
2. Ibid.
3. Dave Balsiger, "Melodyland Christian Center," *Logos Digest,* No. 1, 1973, p. 34.
4. Craig Turner, "The Gospel (With Glitter) According to Rev. Wilkerson," *Los Angeles Times,* April 8, 1979, Part X, p. 12.
5. Ibid., p. 10.
6. Brian Bird, "Melodyland Makes a Comeback," *Charisma,* August, 1987, pp. 58, 60.

Chapter 3

1. Russell Chandler, "When Is a Church Not a Church?" Copyright, 1979, *Los Angeles Times,* Feb. 19, 1979, p. 1. Reprinted by permission.
2. Information from *The Christian Legal Society Newsletter*
3. Michael Seiler, "Church-State Clashes," *Los Angeles Times,* February 11, 1979, p. 32.
4. U.S. Supreme Court (Cantwell v. Connecticut, 1940).
5. Charles M. Whelan, "The Definitional Problems," *Fordham Law Review of 1977,* vol. 45 (New York: Fordham University, 1978), p. 1.
6. Malcolm Muggeridge, *The End of Christendom* (Grand Rapids: William B. Eerdmans Publishing Co., 1980), p. 13.

Chapter 4

1. William Dick, "Millions Can Avoid Income Tax Through Legal Loophole," *National Enquirer,* Jan. 2, 1975, p. 4.
2. Ibid.
3. Ibid.
4. *Tax Court Memo,* 1978-149.
5. Internal Revenue Service News Release, IR-1930.
6. *Internal Revenue Manual,* 7(10)69 pp. 321.^{3}:(3) and 321:3(4).
7. *What Is a Church—The Dilemma of the Para-Church.* The Center for Law and Religious Freedom, p. 25.
8. Internal Revenue Service—Letter 1000(00)(4-77).
9. IRS Letter dated March 28, 1978, to Redlands Bible Church.
10. Mayo Mohs, *Money,* p. 56.

Chapter 5

1. *Your Federal Income Tax,* Publication 17, rev. Nov., 1986, ch. 28, p. 127.
2. "Toward Ethical Fundraising," *Christianity Today,* May 20, 1987, p. 50.
3. David L. McKenna, "Financing the Great Commission," *Christianity Today,* May 15, 1987, pp. 29-30.
4. Eugene B. Habecker, "Biblical Guidelines for Asking and Giving," *Christianity Today,* May 15, 1987, p. 34.

Chapter 6

1. John Sherrill, "Going the Second Mile," *Charisma,* March, 1987, pp. 32-36.
2. Richard N. Ostling, "Enterprising Evangelism," *Time* Magazine, August 3, 1987, p. 53.
3. Taken from *The Golden Cow* by John White. © 1979 John White and used by permission of InterVarsity Press. Downers Grove, IL 60515.
4. From FREEDOM UNDER SIEGE by Madaline Murray O'Hair. Copyright © New York: J.P. Tarcher, Inc., 1974), p. 209 and reprinted with permission of Jeremy P. Tarcher, Inc.

Chapter 7

1. Clifton E. Ohmstead, *The History of Religion in the United States* (Englewood Cliffs, NJ: Prentice Hall, Inc., 1960), p. 218.
2. A. Mervyn Davies, *Foundation of American Freedom* (Nashville: Abingdon Press, 1955), p. 235.
3. Elwin A. Smith, *Religious Liberty in the United States*, Philadelphia: Fortress Press, 1972), p. 252.
4. Evers v. Board of Education, 330 U.U.S. 1 (1947).
5. Albert Werminghoff, article translated from German work, 1907, p. 87.

Chapter 8

1. Earl L. Wingo, *The Illegal Trial of Jesus* (New York: Bobbs-Merrill Co., Inc., 1962), p. 47.
2. Kenneth Scott Lauterette, *The History of Christianity*, vol. 2 (New York: Harper & Row Publishers, 1975).

Chapter 9

1. "A Nation of Advice," *U.S. News & World Report*, March 24, 1987, pp. 65-69.

Postscript

1. "Test for Big Churches," *U.S. News & World Report*, p. 43.
2. Ibid., p. 45.
3. "Quotes of the Week," *U.S. News & World Report*, p. 13.
4. "Washington Whispers," *U.S. News & World Report*, May 25, 1987, p. 17.
5. Jeff Prugh and Russell Chandler, "Old-Time Religion in the Big Time," *Los Angeles Times*, May 20, 1979, p. 1.
6. Ibid., pp. 10-11.
7. Jamie Buckingham, "Phony Christians," *Charisma*, September, 1984, p. 156.